MATERIALS IN PROGRESS

Innovations for Designers and Architects

MATERIALS
IN PROGRESS

Innovations for Designers and Architects

Sascha Peters   Diana Drewes

Birkhäuser
Basel

Graphic design and cover design
Tom Unverzagt, Leipzig

Layout and typesetting
Heike Strempel, Berlin

Editorial supervision and project management
Henriette Mueller-Stahl, Berlin

Translation from German
Julian Reisenberger, Weimar

Production
Heike Strempel, Berlin

Lithography
bildpunkt Druckvorstufen GmbH, Berlin

Paper
120 g/m² Tauro Offset

Printing and binding
Gutenberg Beuys Feindruckerei GmbH

Library of Congress Control Number: 2019936744

Bibliographic information published by the German National Library
The German National Library lists this publication in the Deutsche Nationalbibliografie; detailed bibliographic data are available on the Internet at http://dnb.dnb.de.

ISBN 978-3-0356-1358-2
e-ISBN (PDF) 978-3-0356-1370-4
German Print-ISBN 978-3-0356-1357-5

© 2019 Birkhäuser Verlag GmbH, Basel
P.O. Box 44, 4009 Basel, Switzerland
Part of Walter de Gruyter GmbH, Berlin/Boston

9 8 7 6 5 4 3 2 1

www.birkhauser.com

FOREWORD

Innovations in the materials we use have influenced the development of mankind since time immemorial. New materials are constantly triggering major changes in society, the environment and technology. Today, 70% of all product innovations are attributed to new findings in materials science and a new generation of products is emerging that exploits new functionality made possible by materials research. At the same time, researchers are constantly extending the boundaries of what is feasible and creating materials that will have an important impact on our everyday lives. We are currently on the verge of major new technological advances that will have a disruptive effect on many sectors, whether mobility, consumption or energy supply. As such, material developments point the way forward in many different respects.

In industry, materials are needed that require far fewer resources than was the case 20 years ago, that can fulfil multiple functions, are lighter, thinner, denser and mechanically stronger and also support the potential of a digitalised world. Designers and architects, in turn, frequently deal with questions of sustainability and the impending scarcity of resources and are developing their own material solutions that are founded on bio-based recyclables or waste from other industries and can be fed back into material cycles when a product's life cycle comes to an end. In the process, approaches previously of limited applicability for industrial mass production are being rediscovered and revived through new processing techniques such as additive production. The artisanal know-how of old crafts techniques or knowledge of locally available plants or useful waste material that was previously passed down from generation to generation are experiencing a renaissance.

In recent years, designers have increasingly turned to developing their own material innovations to realise product ideas and production and disposal goals that they were not able to achieve using what was available on the market. This renewed focus on materials has given rise to a new field of activity for designers that in turn has spawned numerous new developments. In many cases, their work is several years ahead of application scenarios in industry and one can expect to see industry adopt some of the methods in the coming years. Achieving greater functionality with fewer means, lower CO_2 emissions in production and disposal, less waste and disposable plastics and more effective material cycles are goals that can help foster and positively influence important social trends and developments such as the transition to new modes of energy production and mobility, the digitalisation of our various living environments and the increasing urbanisation of society.

Finally, with this book we hope to provide you, the reader, with much inspiration and stimulation for new ideas of your own!

Diana Drewes and Sascha Peters

THE NEW MINDFUL-NESS AND CONSCIOUS CONSUMPTION

For many people in the Western world, shopping is one of the most popular leisure activities. On average, every European owns some 10,000 belongings, and that number continues to rise. For economists, rising consumption is a positive trend: it strengthens the economy, creates jobs and increases social security contributions to the public purse. Ecologists, however, view this much more critically, especially in the context of the growing global population. After all, our planet is not growing with it. Natural resources such as water, soil, air and forests are finite, but these resources are part of every single product consumed. In addition, considerable energy is required for their production, use and ultimately for their disposal, too.

Concepts that help us grasp the complexity of these interrelationships such as the ecological footprint or the ecological rucksack, which express the consumption of resources in relation to the end product in kilograms, show us what has been a fact for more than 40 years: we consume more resources than the earth provides and emit more CO_2 than nature is able to decompose. The ecological footprint – the biologically productive area necessary to sustain our lifestyle – grows exponentially with population growth. Biological capacity, on the other hand, has improved only slightly despite technical advances. The consequences are well-known and omnipresent: soil and water pollution, drought, water scarcity and a loss of biodiversity. In Germany alone, every citizen consumes on average twice as many resources as he or she would be entitled to. This is a huge problem, for which solutions must be found.

Festival site with recyclable
cardboard tents in England
Source: Papertent

In vitro bred balls of minced
meat
Source: Memphis Meats

In Europe, a trend towards "meaningful consumption" is emerging, especially among younger generations with families. People are beginning to call into question status symbols such as a car of one's own, or whether one needs a new car or a wardrobe well-stocked with the latest fashion. New concepts for sustainable ways of living instead focus on finding the right balance.

As with all new and innovative approaches towards living sustainably and responsibly, it entails that we reassess what we do for the sake of convenience. But it also requires overcoming bureaucratic hurdles, which in Europe are not insignificant. The various new initiatives that are emerging – the use of biodegradable packaging, the advent of burgers made of insects, a ban on plastic bags and disposable plastic articles, the rise in car-sharing or the use of individual reuseable cups – are also the product of the reform of food and hygiene regulations and innovations in parking space management regulations which local authorities, and in some cases the European Parliament, have implemented to pave the way towards a more sustainable way of life in Europe.

Animal proteins – breeding
mealworms in 18 days
Source: LivinFarms

ALTERNATIVE NUTRITION CONCEPTS

Street food market in New
York City
Source: Haute Innovation

In the last five decades, global meat production has quadrupled. Europeans now consume an annual average of 64 kg of meat per person each year. Researchers expect that rising prosperity in the densely populated emerging economies combined with the trend towards a "Western diet" will lead to a further increase in per capita meat consumption. Food technologists have been developing sustainable meat substitutes for several years, predominantly based on vegetable protein sources such as sweet lupins or algae, but also on more unusual animal protein sources such as insects or jellyfish. The objective is to avoid a one-sided diet that is low in nutrients. As technical advances are made and our understanding of the complex interrelationships of a variety of materials improves, disruptive methods (i.e. methods that may disrupt traditional production processes) such as meat cultivated in vitro (Latin: in glass) are offering increasingly viable solutions to the need for animal proteins. The laboratory cultivation of meat requires far fewer resources, reducing the need for agricultural land and water and, in the case of farmed beef in particular, potentially achieving a hundredfold reduction in climate-damaging methane emissions.

In vitro bred balls of minced meat

Source: Memphis Meats

IN VITRO MEAT

In early 2016, the US start-up Memphis Meats presented to the press a ball of minced meat costing almost 985 euros. What made it special was that it was not made of meat from a slaughtered animal but had been grown in a laboratory. Based on muscle cells from a living cow, it was cultivated on a collagen culture enriched with nutrients such as sugar, amino acids, minerals and vitamins with the addition of a growth serum from the blood of living bovine embryos. This biotechnological process is called tissue engineering and has already proven valuable in the breeding of skin transplants for burn victims in medicine. In contrast to plant cells, animal cells are much more difficult to cultivate. In addition to a sophisticated composition of nutrients and minerals, muscle cells also require weak but regular electrical stimulation to grow and form a thin layer. The membranes can then be minced and dyed with beetroot juice or saffron and enriched with fat. Critics point to the high cost of production and the ethically questionable nature of laboratory meat production: the extraction of the growth serum from the beating heart of an embryo often costs it its life. A new, more cost-effective and ethically justifiable alternative is the use of growth serums made from algae.

Insect burger by
Bugfoundation
Source: Bugfoundation GmbH

BUXBURGER

For more than two billion people around the world, insects are a normal part of their diet. Locusts, worms and crickets are particularly popular in Asia and Africa due to their high protein content and cost-effective production. In Germany, the last known entomophagic recipe, Maikäfersuppe (cockchafer soup), has all but disappeared despite being very popular until the middle of the 20th century. But insects are increasingly making their way back into the European cuisine as a source of protein. The numerous start-ups that are emerging, for example the Bugfoundation or SWARM Protein in Germany or Fazer in Finland, do not, in contrast to other cultures, use recognisable insects for their food creations but instead prefer to use the pulverised product. Insect flour can be used in many ways, for example for baked goods, pasta dough, energy bars or burger patties. As early as 2013, the UN Food and Agriculture Organisation (FAO) drew attention to the advantages of insect-based nutrition. In contrast to livestock such as cows, pigs or chickens, insect production consumes only a fraction of water, land and feed. The rapid growth and uncomplicated raising of cold-blooded animals or ectotherms likewise result in lower greenhouse gas emissions. Ectotherms, unlike poikilotherms, do not need to ingest so much food to acquire energy. A further advantage is the higher percentage of edible insect mass – about 80% – compared with that of cows, where the proportion is only around 40%. Insects are also a healthier alternative to conventional meat from a nutritional point of view. Crickets, for example, are considered to be particularly high in protein and rich in healthy fatty acids and minerals. Nutritionists note, however, that people with crustacean allergies should also be careful with insect consumption.

Crawling protein bomb –
insects are the superfood of
the future
Source: LivinFarms

Mealworm breeding box for
the home kitchen
Source: LivinFarms

The Austrian industrial designer Katharina Unger has launched the first miniature breeding farm for food insects. Her product "The Hive" provides the optimal conditions to breed mealworms within 18 days in one's own kitchen without requiring a lot of space or energy. The latest model is not only attractive and space-saving in its design, but also provides accompanying information for the new mealworm breeder. It explains the advantages of the nutritional concept and provides a step-by-step guide to feeding the insects with organic waste such as vegetable skins and fruit peel, introducing younger consumers to the superfood of the future in a playful manner.

Jellyfish chips – a fishy snack from the sea
Source: Mie Thorborg Pedersen/ University of Southern Denmark

JELLYFISH CHIPS

Danish gastrophysicist Mie Thorborg Pedersen has discovered a potential food source for the future in the form of the jellyfish that live around the Danish coast. The particular species of jellyfish is non-toxic and very easy to catch, but rather than landing on a plate, as they might in China, the slithery jellyfish are processed into crunchy crisps. To extract the water from this unusual seafood, the scientist developed a customised dehydration process. To break down the water-storing collagen that gives the jellyfish its form, it is soaked in alcohol for approximately 48 hours. The alcoholic bath gives the jellyfish a more solid, rubbery consistency and causes its transparent colour to become milky. To achieve a satisfying crunchiness, the alcohol is then evaporated in a commercial drying oven. According to the young researcher, jellyfish crisps melt almost instantaneously in the mouth leaving behind a slightly salty aftertaste.

SWEET LUPINS

Scientists at the Fraunhofer Institute in Freising have been working for several years on future plant-based alternatives to traditional dairy products. Back in 2014, they were able to successfully produce yoghurt from the protein-rich seeds of domestic sweet lupins, once they had succeeded in developing a method to extract the unpleasantly bitter and grassy taste from the plant mass. Lupins are comparatively undemanding plants that will grow on nutrient-poor soils and are considered the European counterpart to soy plants. The scientists were also able to develop ice cream using a concentrate derived from the protein-rich plant. Andrea Hickisch, one of the scientists at the laboratory kitchen in Freising, has gone a step further and is currently endeavouring to make matured lupin products such as cheese, which is no easy task: in contrast to fresh produce such as yoghurt or cream cheese, mature cheese production requires the appropriate microorganisms to initiate a successful fermentation process and create the right structure.

Noodles made of cellulose and konjac root
Source: Haute Innovation

Camembert made of almond milk
Source: Haute Innovation

CAMEMBERT MADE OF NUTS

In addition to working with sweet lupins, Andrea Hickisch from the Fraunhofer Institute in Freising also sees great potential for developing food using nuts such as almonds, pistachios or cashew kernels to create dairy products from plant-based materials. Initial attempts to produce Camembert cheese from almonds appear promising. Ground almonds were first boiled in water at 90°C and after the nut-water mixture had cooled, the milky liquid was inoculated with edible moulds and acidifying agents to cultivate a taste that approaches that of an aromatic Camembert. Although not all testers were convinced by the initial round of taste tests, a first step has been made.

CELLULOSE NOODLES

A few years ago, the Japanese textile company Omikenshi Co. from Osaka surprised the market by expanding into the food industry. Now, in addition to their textiles, they sell extremely low-fat, cellulose-based noodles made of the same raw material they use for their textiles. To transform the cellulose material into an edible flour, the company developed its own production process that combines the cellulose with konjac root, which is similar to a sweet potato. The low-carbohydrate noodles are aimed not only at health-conscious Japanese consumers but also, for example, at the Chinese market, where increasing prosperity has brought with it an accompanying rise in obesity.

Baker's Butchery – from industrial bread overproduction to mealworm protein
Source: Lukas Keller

CONCEPTS FOR REDUCING FOOD WASTE

According to the Federal Ministry of Food and Agriculture, every German discarded an average of 55 kg of food in 2017. Of that a good 34 % was made up of fruit and vegetables, followed by cooked food leftovers with a share of 16 % and bread and bakery products amounting to 14 %. In recent years, more and more developers have found creative ways of addressing the problem and have developed strategies of their own to tackle the problem of food waste.

MEALWORM CHIPS

Baker's Butchery – chips made of stale bread and mealworms
Source: Lukas Keller

As part of the "reuse" semester project at Burg Giebichenstein in Halle, the designer Lukas Keller has developed an exciting concept for reusing stale bread from industrial bakeries. Entitled "Baker's Butchery", his concept combines the up-and-coming theme of insects as the protein source of the future with stale bread from large bakeries, which is often thrown away due to overproduction. Although insect breeding is far less demanding than cattle breeding, requiring less space and much less feed, it is important to keep the temperature at approximately 30 °C for efficient breeding. An obvious solution is to direct unused waste heat from the bakery to a nearby breeding house to provide the optimum growth conditions. The combination of crushed stale bread and mealworms is also a sensible idea: the chitin contained in the exoskeleton of the mealworms has a gelling and binding effect and lends the new chips the necessary stability. The first product by the designer is mealworm chips, which he coloured with beetroot juice.

The fruit rescuers of Berlin –
a healthy snack made from
unsaleable fruit
Source: Dörrwerk

DÖRRWERK BERLIN

With his concept of the "Dörrwerk" factory, Zubin Farahani from Berlin has come up with a solution for the large amounts of food that many supermarkets and wholesalers in Germany throw away. Every day, huge amounts of apples, pineapples, mangos and other fruit are discarded because they either have small flaws or are overripe. In particular, tropical fruit that ripens faster is often disposed of, according to the young entrepreneur. But as brown stains or small dents have no influence on the taste of the sweet suppliers of vitamins, the fruit can still be processed. Farahani's concept uses the traditional technique of drying to not only create a sustainable and healthy snack, but also save enormous amounts of fruit from disposal or the biogas plant. The dried, wafer-thin crisps made of fruit are sold online and in selected supermarkets under the name "Fruchtpapier". The basis for each type of fruit paper is apple purée, which makes the fruit paper soft and tasty, to which a few drops of lemon juice and various types of fruit are added, depending on the desired flavour, before being spread in thin layers for the drying process.

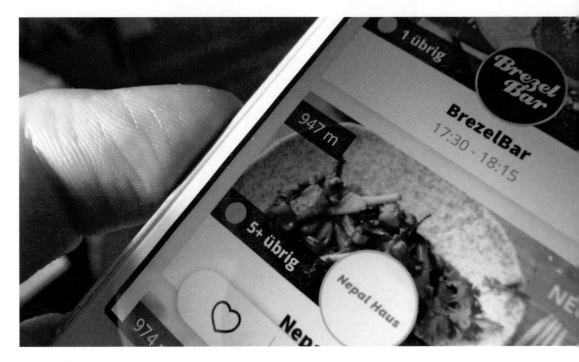

App to avoid food waste
Source: Haute Innovation

"TOO GOOD TO GO" APP

The "Too Good to Go" app offers restaurants and cafés a digital platform through which to sell their remaining prepared food shortly before closing time. The idea recalls the sales tactics of market traders who sell off their remaining goods at dumping prices shortly before shutting in order to avoid the logistics and cost of disposing of them. Both retailers and consumers benefit. As it is usually impossible to say exactly how much will be left over, the quantities are given in so-called food boxes or portions and offered online at a greatly reduced fixed price. Using the app, customers can conveniently peruse nearby restaurants and their offers and buy portions online before arriving at the store to pick them up in a fixed time frame shortly before closing time. The only drawback with the service is the uncertainty: if the goods are indeed sold contrary to expectations, the journey was in vain and the money is refunded online. But for those who are flexible and open to surprises, it can be a ticket to very reasonably priced sushi, sandwiches or fresh salads and smoothies, and at the same time saves food from being thrown away.

REUSABLE RATHER
THAN DISPOSABLE

After free plastic bags were successfully banned from supermarkets in numerous countries, the coffee-to-go cup has since become the symbol of the throwaway society in the Western world and is a common sight on the street. More and more end consumers are, however, beginning to change their ways and have started to use returnable or reusable cups in an effort to protect the environment, and sellers are increasingly rewarding them accordingly by reducing the price of takeaway hot drinks.

WEDUCER

The Berlin-based designer Julian Lechner has come up with several surprising creations. Using dried coffee grounds and a lignin-based binding agent, he not only makes espresso and cappuccino cups, but also a returnable cup with a screw-top lid: a positive example of how readily available urban waste material can be used to produce a waste-reducing product. All variants are available from his online shop.

Weducer Cup – a takeaway
coffee cup made of coffee
grounds
Source: Kaffeeform / Julian Lechner

Tavolina – a porcelain
drinking bottle
Source: Peter Eichler / Saale-Land

TAVOLINA – A PORCELAIN DRINKING BOTTLE

The trend towards reusable receptacles is also making inroads into the market for water bottles. Designs for reusable bottles are just as varied as the materials they are made of, which include glass, stainless steel or plastic. Melamine bottles are particularly popular in Asia because they are unbreakable, light and inexpensive. However, even at temperatures as low as 70 °C, they can release melamine and formaldehyde into the beverage. The product designer Claudia Bischoff at Eschenbach Porzellan has presented an alternative drinking bottle that is pollutant-free, food-safe and above all robust. The bottle called TAVOLINA Aqua is made of hard porcelain and is dishwasher- and microwave-safe. The lid is made of thermoplastic elastomers (TPE) and polypropylene (PP) and is free of harmful bisphenol A (BPA).

WATER REFILLING STATIONS

Those who want to refill their water bottles free of charge can download a mobile phone app by the non-profit organisation Refill Deutschland. It shows a virtual map with all participating water refill points in the vicinity, which can be restaurants, cafés and drinking water fountains.

Compostable water bottle
made of algae gelatine
Source: Ari Jónsson

BIODEGRADABLE PACKAGING

Assuming that in future animal-based food will be produced outside cities and plant-based food on roofs or vertical gardens in urban conurbations, product groups such as packaging will play an increasingly important role in closing biological material cycles in cities. It is important in this context to clarify what biodegradability means: the industrial processing of organic waste is often mistakenly equated with decomposition via conventional composting.

ASPIC BOTTLES

The Icelandic product designer Ari Jónsson has developed a water bottle that rots within a few days of use. A mixture of agar-agar and water is brought to the boil to initiate the gelling process and then, once it has acquired a jelly-like consistency, the viscous material is poured into a mould. After cooling, a transparent shiny film forms on its surface. In physics, this phenomenon is known as syneresis: water is released from the surface of the gelled structure but does not weaken it. When the bottle is refilled with water, the film inside the bottle is retained, ensuring its continued stability. The outside, on the other hand, dries out after a while, and the material becomes brittle.

Compostable packaging
made of plant waste
Source: BIO-LUTIONS International AG

Compostable packaging
made from locally available
agricultural waste material
Source: Screenshot from the
YouTube-Video / BIO-LUTIONS –
Agricultural Waste to Biodegradable
Cartons & Tableware

COMPOSTABLE PACKAGING MADE FROM
BANANA AND SUGAR CANE LEAVES

The Hamburg-based start-up Bio-Lutions shows how sustainable packaging can be.
Its 100 % compostable packaging is made directly at the place of production in India
from banana and sugar cane leaves, a waste product of the food-producing industry.
Until now, the unused, dried leaves of sugar cane grass and harvested banana palms
were simply burnt. The German company now purchases the former waste by-product
from the farmers at fair prices and uses it to produce biodegradable cardboard packaging for fruit and vegetables in a local factory. Since the required binder is already
present in the plant residues, all that is needed is the addition of water to produce
stable packaging cardboard.

Biodegradable and pollutant-free packaging made of wood and a natural binder from Finland

Source: Sulapac

PACKED IN WOOD

The Finnish company Sulapac has launched an environmentally friendly alternative to conventional plastic packaging for cosmetics and other wood-based hygiene products using material from sustainably managed Nordic forests, which is readily available and free of harmful substances. The raw material is first shredded into wood chips and heated together with a binding agent. While the company has not revealed which binder is used, it is known that it protects the wood from burning. After heating, the mass can be shaped using conventional methods such as injection moulding. Its significantly lower CO_2 footprint and low price make it a serious contender for use in place of its petrochemical predecessors. The only disadvantage is its limited stability of approximately twelve months.

Edible takeaway tableware
at a market in Samarkand/
Uzbekistan
Source: Haute Innovation

EDIBLE PACKAGING

According to the latest statistics, Europeans produce on average about 31 kg of plastic packaging waste every year, a figure so alarming that the European Parliament has since passed a law banning disposable plastic tableware from 2020 onwards. In the Anthropocene age, in which man shapes his environment, this represents a significant attempt at living more responsibly for the benefit of future generations. Ideas for edible packaging as a potential replacement of conventional packaging have so far ranged from the good old ice-cream waffle cones to edible straws made of sugar. The newest developments go a step further and only use raw materials that do not compete directly with the traditional food-producing industry.

ALGAE PACKAGING

Water-soluble food-packaging material based on algae
Source: EVOWARE

According to EVOWARE, the packaging of the future is floating in the sea. The Indonesian company has developed compostable and edible packaging based on algae for dry products such as pasta, spices and even burgers. The packaging has no flavour, is free of preservatives and can last up to two years in a cool and dry environment. It can easily be dissolved in warm water and can even be eaten.

Edible mouthful of water to avoid waste at big events
Source: Ohoo

OHOO

In late 2015, one of the most unusual water bottles in the world was launched, causing a small sensation in the media. Looking much like a soap bubble filled with water, it is soft and completely edible. The media are already heralding it as the bottle of the future. Although countries like Germany have long attempted to minimise everyday plastic waste by introducing a bottle deposit, 46 % of all beverage bottles are still disposable bottles. Irrespective of whether the bottle is truly practical for everyday use, the edible packaging made of water, alginate and calcium could massively reduce the waste problem at large events such as concerts, festivals and sporting events. The chemical structure of alginate is similar to that of plant starch and is also used as a thickening agent in the food industry. It is classed as a long-chain molecule or polymer, which, in conjunction with calcium ions, cross-links to form a three-dimensional sponge network that can absorb water. The natural reaction of both components has been known for years in the field of molecular cuisine as "spherification" and is used to encapsulate liquids. Liquids enriched with sodium alginate are dripped into a salt solution and, due to the calcium ions they contain, form an edible gel shell within a few minutes that is similar to the skin of a grape. The edible water drops can be stored in clear water until ready to be consumed.

Spoontainable – a sustainable, edible ice-cream spoon
Source: Spoontainable

VEGAN ICE-CREAM SPOON WITHOUT SUGAR

A group of young students from near Stuttgart have found inspiration in the waste bins of the food-processing industry. Using discarded fruit peel, they have developed an edible ice-cream spoon, which they are already selling under the name of "Spoon-tainable" and is even available in various flavours such as chocolate, vanilla or straw-berry. The primary component of the edible spoon is dried plant fibres from fruit peel, ground into a flour and then pressed into shape using a process much like baking biscuits. Their creation has met with great interest and the first contracts with local ice-cream shops are due to be signed in early 2019.

Edible packaging film made
of milk proteins
Source: Jonas Emil Arndt

FOOD-SAFE COATINGS

A completely new market in edible coatings and packaging films has now emerged that not only contributes to reducing the use of plastics for packaging but also helps perishable products such as fruit remain fresh for longer, increasing the profit margin on sales. The newest developments have nothing in common with the first generation of starch-based films, which protected its contents inadequately, impacting on their shelf life. The new coatings comprise natural substances that nature can work with, and also increase the shelf life of perishable foods many times over. This pattern of innovation recalls the history of cellophane film, the first transparent packaging film used for food. From 1930 onwards, the synthetic material made of 100% renewable raw materials was used for packaging food. At that time, it was similar in composition to a viscose fibre and could be composted or disposed of with waste paper. Over time, however, expectations shifted as to what a transparent packaging material should fulfil. It was combined with petroleum-based plastics, signalling an end to its environmental compatibility in the long term. To prevent this pattern repeating itself, we need the expertise not just of chemists, but above all also of biologists.

Protective edible coating
for spraying on sensitive
foodstuffs
Source: Haute Innovation

Thin packaging foil made of
the milk protein casein
Source: Jonas Emil Arndt

EDIBLE CASEIN FOIL

US Department of Agriculture (USDA) researchers have developed a new generation of edible food films that has attracted interest in industry. Using milk proteins, they produced a casein film that can shield perishable foods from oxygen up to 500 times better than its petroleum-based predecessor, thus keeping food fresh for longer. After the first experiments showed that the film dissolves much too quickly in water, the researchers went in search of natural additives that could improve the strength of the thin membrane along with its resistance to moisture. Tests proved successful with pectin, a vegetable polysaccharide that gives plant parts such as fruit peel the requisite strength and water-regulating properties.

EDIBLE PROTECTIVE COATING MADE OF PLANT MATERIAL

Apeel Sciences, a start-up from California, has developed a protective edible coating for soft fruits and vegetables. It is tasteless, low in calories and is derived from plant material such as pear stalks, fruit peel, seeds and so on. The spray-on edible coating is composed primarily of glycerol phosphatide, a substance that contributes to the formation of the bio-membranes of higher plants, and that occurs naturally as vegetable lipids in liquid or solid form as fats. Due to their molecular structure, the odourless and tasteless lipids are insoluble in water and offer lasting protection against moisture and gases that would otherwise massively accelerate the ripening process. As such, the coating greatly improves the quality of the product for consumers. This could mean that in future, bananas or tomatoes can be harvested once fully ripe and still be transported economically to the end consumer before becoming over-ripe. Fresh produce would not need to be cooled so much during transport, saving costs and reducing its CO_2 footprint.

ERADICATING MICROPLASTICS

Electron microscope image of cellulose particles made of beechwood that are now being used in various care products

Source: Fraunhofer IMWS

Microplastics have now been found in natural environments all over the world, in the oceans and their inhabitants, in the Antarctic, in almost all major rivers, in the mountains and even in the soil. In human beings, too, plastic particles, some as large as 5 mm, have been detected in the digestive system and even in blood. The origins of the widely travelled microplastics can be traced back to a variety of industries. In a new study, the Fraunhofer Institute for Environmental, Safety and Energy Technology in Oberhausen, Germany, has identified 51 sources. According to the scientists, one third of the 330,000 t of microplastics produced per year in Germany (approximately 4 kg per German citizen per year) can be attributed to abrasion from car tyres. Another source is sewage sludge from sewage treatment plants that is used as a biofertiliser in agriculture but is contaminated with plastic particles. With each washing cycle, thousands of small plastic fibres from synthetic clothing such as polyester, viscose or acrylic are washed down the drain and collect in sewage sludge. Abrasion from sports and playground surfaces, shoe soles and road markings is a further source. Plastic waste already adrift at sea and in landfill sites on land also decomposes into smaller and smaller particles and is distributed as secondary plastic by currents and wind across the planet. In the USA, Canada, New Zealand, Great Britain and since July 2018 also in Sweden, another source of microplastics has been identified and banned by legislators: cosmetic and care products such as skin creams, toothpaste or shower gels containing microbeads may no longer be sold. For decades, microplastics have been specially produced as a primary plastic for use in abrasives and peeling agents as well as an additive and filler in the cosmetics and detergent industries.

Cellulose particles from beechwood could in future replace microplastics as abrasives in toothpaste
Source: Haute Innovation

Seashells as a natural alternative to microplastic abrasives
Source: Haute Innovation

BIODEGRADABLE ABRASIVES FOR TOOTHPASTES

In numerous cosmetic and body care products, natural abrasives, binders and fillers such as crushed seashells and eggshells, salts or powdered stone and carbon powder have been replaced by cheap and plentiful microplastics. The Fraunhofer Institute for Microstructure of Materials and Systems (IMWS) in Halle is developing an environmentally friendly and biodegradable substitute as part of a research project. The scientists presented cellulose particles made of beechwood, oats, wheat and maize with a view to manufacturing them as cost-effectively as possible. The development work focused primarily on toothpastes and body scrubs. In order to replicate the size, shape, hardness and surface structure of the microplastic particles previously used, the various cellulose particles were continuously refined in over 24 months of research work. Particularly promising results were achieved with optimised beechwood particles for toothpastes, providing good cleaning performance on the very sensitive tooth surface. Further tests with walnut, apricot and olive-stone shells will follow.

Using eggshells and tomato skins can reduce particulate matter abrasion from car tyres
Source: Haute Innovation

ADDITIVES FROM TOMATO SKINS AND EGGSHELLS

Research colleagues from Ohio succeeded in minimising the additives used for the production of car tyres, which until now were mostly petroleum-based and together constitute up to 30 % of most commercially available tyres. One such additive is industrially produced carbon black, which is used as a colouring agent and to strengthen the rubber material. However, longer durability and improved rolling properties also come at the cost of more particulate matter released by the tyres when driving. An alternative additive is eggshells, which have a microporous surface. Tomato skins have also been successfully tested. This combination of easily available and abundant waste materials from food production particularly surprised the researchers at Ohio. They identified an optimal composition of carbon black, eggshells and tomato skins that makes the rubber firmer while at the same time retaining the necessary flexibility.

Can moth larvae simply eat up our plastic waste problem?
Source: Haute Innovation

PLASTIC-EATING ORGANISMS

Chance observations are sometimes the origin of unexpected breakthroughs in science, thus providing answers to difficult questions that have preoccupied mankind for decades such as the question of how to dispose of plastic waste. Many industrially produced plastics are not degradable and are increasingly polluting our planet, a development that in recent years has prompted ever more intensive research into environmentally friendly ways of decomposing plastic. The breadth of research approaches is reflected in the variety of options, which range from insects to fungi and bacteria.

PLASTIC-DECOMPOSING WAX MOTHS

Why a good moth is not necessarily a dead moth was discovered by chance by Federica Bertocchini when inspecting her beehives in Santander, Spain. After clearing an infested beehive of greater wax moth maggots, she was surprised to discover that the parasites she had collected in a plastic bag had eaten their way to freedom within a few minutes. She soon suspected that the small white maggots (Latin: *Galleria mellonella*) could eat polyethylene (PE) plastic film. Subsequent research into this sensational discovery led to the identification of an enzyme in the animal's intestine that the scientists believe can decompose the plastic. Other researchers were, however, unable to corroborate their findings in further tests, and control experiments ultimately showed that the worms simply excreted the chemically unchanged plastic as microplastic particles.

34

Insects with a craving for plastic
Source: Haute Innovation

MEALWORMS

In Oberhausen in Germany, scientists have high hopes that another small gobbler, the mealworm, can offer a possible solution. According to the researchers, mealworms have a ravenous appetite for polystyrene. The creature's intestines contain various bacteria that enable them not only to eat polystyrene without dying, but also to digest and decompose it. The worms can thereafter be kept in the biological cycle as fish food.

PLASTIC-EATING BACTERIUM

In 2016, Japanese researchers discovered a plastic-eating bacterium in a PET bottle recycling plant. The scientists suspect that a mutation has led to the formation of the enzyme PETease, making it possible for the bacterium to digest plastic. At the University of Portsmouth, research colleagues took a detailed look at the structure of the bacterium. Using X-rays, they modified the amino acids of the bacteria and slowed down the decomposition process of the plastic. To their astonishment, the opposite happened, and the effectiveness of the bacterium was further optimised. Although much research has still to be conducted before such bacteria can be put into practice, the scientists are optimistic about future applications.

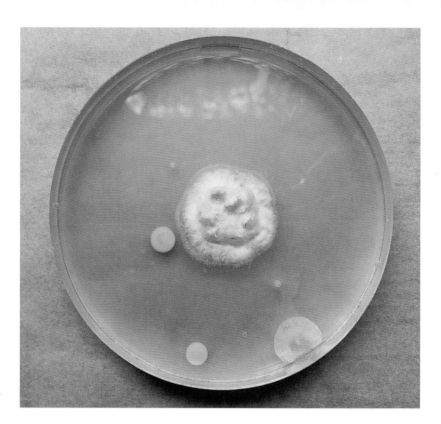

Plastic-decomposing fungus
Source: Haute Innovation

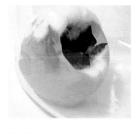

The "Fungi Mutarium" con-
cept – a fungus decomposes
plastic into harmless and
even edible components
Source: Katharina Unger & Julia
Kaisinger / LIVIN Studio

FUNGI

Students at Yale University have discovered an extraordinary fungus called "Pestaloti-
opsis microspore" in Ecuador's rainforest that can decompose polyurethane, a plastic
commonly used in construction foams, mattresses, shoe soles and adhesives. It is
well-known that fungi play an important role in the biological cycle through their ability to decompose organic material, but the fact that some species can even decompose plastics or crude oil into non-toxic components and then absorb them is new.
The discovery of the whitish-yellow, fine-grained sponge on the bark of a guava tree
has brought the researchers a step closer to solving the problem of plastic waste.
Unfortunately, legal disputes between Ecuador and the University of Yale over the
ownership of the miracle mushroom have so far hindered the ability to conduct more
rigorous research. A recent legal victory for the South Americans has now enabled the
first research projects to finally proceed and new findings are eagerly awaited.

A compostable tent
Source: James Molkenthin/Comp-a-tent

TEMPORARY HOUSING

For many people, summer time is also music festival time. Festival visitors produce on average up to 15 kg of rubbish, sometimes even leaving behind their tents because they were damaged, too cheap to be worth keeping or simply forgotten in the haze of a hangover. The disposal of the plastic tents is a costly nuisance for the festival organisers, who have to take them to an incinerator.

CARDBOARD TENTS FOR FESTIVALS

Festival site with recyclable cardboard tents in England
Source: Papertent

A potential remedy has been developed by the Dutch company KarTent in the form of cardboard tents. According to the manufacturers, the tents can withstand three days of continuous rain, are 100 % recyclable and incur half as much CO_2 emissions during manufacture as traditional tents. KarTent sells most of their tents directly to festival organisers that want to offer visitors a sustainable short-term camping solution on site for a small fee.

THE COMPOSTABLE TENT

The start-up Comp-a-tent from London has been successfully selling compostable tents for festival use since 2016. According to the founder Amanda Campbell, her bioplastic tent can withstand wind and weather over a festival weekend and can be disposed of in a conventional composting plant. The tent decomposes completely within 120 days. All the components and materials used are compostable: the tent poles are made of paper and the glue used is based on casein or milk. The idea for a biodegradable tent was born when the young British founder helped clean up after the Glastonbury Festival in England. Every year some 20,000 tents are left behind and have to be disposed of at the organiser's expense.

2

SUSTAINABILITY AND THE CIRCULAR ECONOMY

Sneakers made from recycled waste
Source: Ruby Odilia Photo Lab

Every new report on another temperature record, on plastic waste in the oceans or the difficulty of sourcing certain resources is a further sign of our need to radically change our ways as consumers. As the global population rises, it becomes imperative that we reject our culture of disposability in favour of reusing and recycling materials and resources by establishing circular economies. The Club of Rome's "Limits to Growth" report, presented in 1972, first warned of the finite availability of natural resources. The projections published at the time were based on computer simulations by specialists from Massachusetts Institute of Technology (MIT) which predicted that if consumer behaviour remained unchanged, we would expend the world's most important resources within a hundred years, in turn precipitating a drastic decline in the world's population.

Shards wall tiles made of recycled building rubble
Source: Lea Schücking

The start of the first major oil crisis one year later only seemed to confirm their findings. The Arab-Israeli Yom Kippur War and the use of restrictions on oil exports as a lever for political interests culminated in driving bans and deserted motorways. Since then, the scarcity of resources and disputes over the distribution of resources are now said to be the second most frequent cause of conflict in global politics.

The Earth's natural resources are finite. In addition, the world's population is rising. If the patterns of consumption and lifestyle of the Western world continue to spread to other regions, we will expend them even more quickly. Companies such as Deep Space Industries from Luxembourg or Planetary Resource from the USA are also aware

Cellulose from denim waste is reconstituted into aerogel
Source: Donna Squire / deakin

Information panel on recycling at a tea factory in Sri Lanka
Source: Haute Innovation

of this and hope in the not-too-distant future to mine precious metals and rare minerals from asteroids. Similar asteroid-mining enterprises have likewise succeeded in attracting prominent billionaires such as Google co-founder Larry Page and the filmmaker James Cameron as investors. Whether their idea will pay off economically remains to be seen, and both companies have warned investors of the risk of substantial losses.

Neither of these initiatives, however, address the fact that it is not the absolute lack of resources on earth that threatens our existence but our inefficient use of them. The challenge facing industrial societies in the coming decades lies in making better use of resources and converting industrial production processes to closed material cycles. The shift away from "consuming" towards "using" resources is particularly important for material-intensive sectors, especially in view of the growing world population. Old jeans are now being turned into cartilage implants, building rubble from landfill into high-quality wall tiles and used chewing gum into soles for sneakers.

Recycling is moving towards upcycling, and waste materials are becoming valuable resources, each with their own specific qualities for use in innovative products. The high-quality recyclable materials recovered at the end of one life cycle mark the starting point for the next product life cycle. Our resources could then circulate in biological and technical cycles for as long as is economically sensible and qualitatively possible.

Plastic Whale boat made of recycled plastic
Source: Plastic Whale

Office chair and table lights covered with felt made from ocean plastics
Source: Plastic Whale

OCEAN PLASTICS

1,000 plastic bottles for a table, 60 to 70 for a chair
Source: Plastic Whale

Although researchers found vast quantities of plastic waste floating in the oceans as far back as 1997, scientists estimate that several million tonnes still make their way into the sea every year. In 2010 alone, that figure was reportedly more than 8 million t, which corresponds to five shopping bags per 30 cm of coastline worldwide.

PLASTIC WHALE

Plastic Whale is the world's first professional plastic fishing company. As a social enterprise, its aim is to free the watercourses of the world from plastics and use the material recovered for new products. The company started in Amsterdam in 2011 as an initiative to fish waste such as bags and PET bottles from the canals. From the first 9,000 PET bottles the company founder Marius Smit built himself a boat, which he now uses to offer tourists guided waste-fishing tours through the canals of Amsterdam. Since then, 21,080 plastic fishermen have recovered 195,000 PET bottles and 3,500 sacks of plastic waste from the canals. In collaboration with Lama Concepts and the office furniture manufacturer Vepa, Plastic Whale has designed a sustainable office furniture collection using felt made exclusively of plastic from recycled PET bottles.

40

Hawaii shirt made from ocean plastic
Source: Wieden+Kennedy Amsterdam/Corona

CORONA PARADISE? SHIRT

For the beverage manufacturer Corona and the environmental organisation Parley for the Oceans, the creative agency Wieden + Kennedy from Amsterdam, together with the Spanish designer A. Correa, have designed a shirt to draw attention to the littering of the oceans and beaches. At first glance, the "Paradise? Shirt", as it is called, looks like a colourful Hawaii shirt, but on closer inspection, its pattern reveals itself to consist of images of single-use tableware, six-pack rings and other plastic objects of daily use floating alongside fish and crabs. The limited-edition shirt is made from plastic waste collected by Parley for the Oceans from the sea and on islands and beaches.

POLYAMIDES FROM
FISHING NETS

Billed at the time as the first synthetic fibre in the world, nylon is now used widely
in numerous industries due to its good durability. The fashion industry, for example,
values it for the excellent colouring capacity of nylon fibres for swimwear and stockings. The good abrasion resistance of the fibre surfaces and its chemical resistance
make it an excellent choice for woven floor coverings such as carpets in interiors. But it
is the fishing industry in the USA that has arguably benefitted most from the development of nylon: in the 1960s, the production of fishing nets changed from traditional,
but not very durable, fibrous materials such as hemp, sisal or linen to synthetic nylon,
which is strong and extremely tear-resistant.

50 years on, however, we now know that nylon nets represent a significant portion of
maritime plastic pollution. Sea-dwelling creatures either eat the remains of fishing
nets or get caught in them. EU-funded projects such as MARELITT Baltic have been
tackling this problem for years, recovering remnants of nets still drifting in the Baltic
Sea.

Costa sunglasses are made from fishing nets reclaimed from the sea
Source: Bureo

FROM FISHING TO EYE-CATCHER

The US company Costa Sunglasses is not only a leading producer of high-performance sunglasses but also the initiator of the "Kick Plastic" campaign. The initiative aims to educate people about rising marine plastic pollution and its consequences. In particular, the company has focused on stray fishing nets floating in the sea due to their size, durability and high tensile strength, which makes them particularly dangerous for marine life. According to the company, they account for 10 % of floating plastic waste in the world's oceans. Unlike many other waste particles, polyamide fishing nets can be easily recycled as a pure material. The challenge lies in recovering the material, as the nets are often entwined around rocks, wreckages and other foreign objects, or they float about torn into little pieces. In collaboration with Bureo, recycling specialists for net products, Costa Sunglasses uses waste material recovered from the sea. After cleansing, the nets are processed into small pellets in a mechanical recycling process and then formed into the desired product shape in steel moulds. As part of the "Untangled Collection", the eyewear manufacturer sells glasses frames made of 100 %-recycled nylon nets.

Carpet made from recycled
fishing nets by ROPE HOPE
Source: Sep Verboom/ LIVABLE®

Skateboard made from
fishing nets
Surce: Bureo Skateboards

ROPE RUG

Sustainable design encompasses not just the right choice of materials but also of processing methods, according to the Belgian carpet manufacturer Papilio. The company produces high-quality carpets carefully handcrafted from old nylon nets and ropes from Philippine fishermen. The project unites local recycling initiatives with local handicraft techniques and is presented in detail on the company's LIVABLE® platform.

SKATEBOARD FROM THE SEA

In Chile, 2.8 m² of disused fishing net is enough to make a skateboard. The Americans Ben Kneppers, Kevin Ahearn and David Stover of the net product recycler Bureo collect discarded nets from the beaches of Chile or purchase damaged and unusable nets directly from the fishermen, before preparing them for further processing in the capital, Santiago. The resulting material can be melted and formed into new shapes. "The Minnow" is the young company's first successful product, a trendy skateboard that looks like a fish with a scaly surface for added grip when skateboarding.

A pair of stockings or a bottle made of chicory root may soon become reality, according to scientists at the University of Hohenheim (left: Dominik Wüst; right: Markus Gölz)
Source: University of Hohenheim

BIO-BASED HIGH-PERFORMANCE FIBRES

Synthetic fibres are prized in particular for high-performance products due to their mechanical properties, good damage tolerance and economic advantages over bio-based solutions. But with the increasing depletion of oil reserves, scientists have begun in recent years to search for innovative approaches and new impulses for sustainable alternatives to synthetic high-performance fibres.

NYLON FROM THE CHICORY ROOT

Scientists at the University of Hohenheim are exploiting the by-product of chicory cultivation to produce hydroxymethylfurfural (HMF). HMF is an important chemical base for producing polyamides, polyesters and PET and could therefore replace some of the raw materials used today in the plastics industry that are currently based on crude oil. The chicory root is, according to the researchers, an almost ideal waste material. After harvesting the edible leaves, the root tubers, which make up good 30 % of the plant, are typically disposed of in biogas plants or turned back into the soil to rot. Around 800,000 t of this previously unused resource are produced annually in Europe alone.

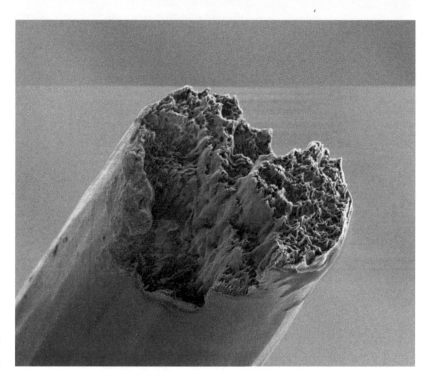

Ultra-strong nanofibres made of cellulose

ULTRA-STRONG CELLULOSE NANOFIBRES

A research team led by Daniel Söderberg from the Royal Institute of Technology (KTH) in Stockholm has been able to produce nanofibres from cellulose with exceptional mechanical strength using the PETRA III X-ray radiation source at the DESY Research Centre in Hamburg. With a tensile stiffness of 86 GPa and a tensile strength of 1.57 GPa, the biodegradable material exceeds the strength of steel and even spider silk. In a process called hydrodynamic focusing, commercially available cellulose nanofibres are assembled to form an ultra-strong macroscopic thread without any additional adhesives. The fibres, which are about 2 to 5 nm thin and up to 700 nm long, are pressed through a 1-mm-wide channel suspended in a carrier fluid. By supplying deionized water and low-pH water from one side, the nanofibres in the channel not only align in the right direction, but also self-organise into a well-packed state, where they join together to form a fibre. The resulting supramolecular forces between the cellulose nanofibers obviate the need for additional adhesives. PETRA III's high-brilliance X-ray beam made it possible to monitor and ultimately optimise the process in detail.

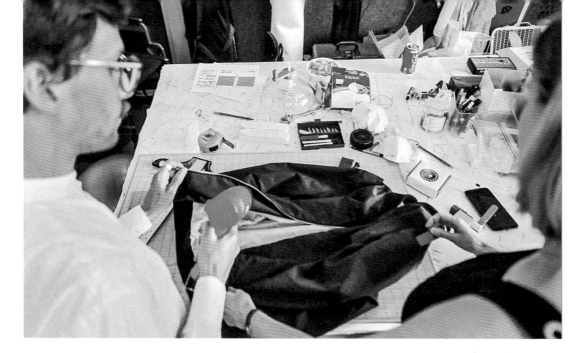

RECYCLABLE TEXTILES

Buttons and zips can be
removed from clothing with
the help of a hairdryer
Source: Resortecs®

Almost every clothing company has inevitably turned its attention to the issue of sustainability in recent years. Whether jackets made from PET bottles, swimwear made of recycled nylon or T-shirts made of organic cotton, numerous sustainable products are already available on the market. Although some have succeeded in creating an almost closed material cycle, recycling resources should not lead to even more consumption. In the fast-fashion sector in particular, sustainable design means practising social responsibility throughout the entire production chain. Producing under fair conditions is just the beginning; the disposal of used clothing and the avoidance of wastage during production are likewise important. Donating clothing to charity, as is widespread in Europe, is increasingly turning out to be an ecological and economic problem for the receiving countries in Africa. In Tanzania, for example, imported second-hand goods have brought the local textile industry to a standstill and have led to overflowing landfill sites. As a consequence, the East African country no longer accepts textile goods.

re:newcell fibres
Source: re:newcell

The yellow dress made from
recycled old textiles
Source: re:newcell

RE:NEWCELL – LOCALLY MADE

In 2014, a yellow dress caused a sensation in the textile industry. The dress presented by the Swedish company re:newcell was the first garment in the world to be made completely of recycled old textiles. The announcement heralded a new method that makes it possible to decompose fabric rests with a high cellulose content such as cotton, viscose or lyocell into cotton-wool-like fibres. In contrast to the high-profile recycling campaign by a well-known Swedish fashion house in 2013, re:newcell's dress is made of 100%-recycled old clothing. The fashion chain used a different process, shredding old textiles into pieces so small that it was no longer possible to make new yarns from them without adding new fibres. Consequently, the fashion chain's garments comprised only 20% recycled cotton. re:newcell's concept proved so convincing that in late 2017 the fashion group decided to cooperate with the Swedish start-up as an investor.

Bowl made of yarn remnants
Source: krupka–stieghan Studio für Produktdesign

Yarn sections from production
Source: krupka–stieghan Studio für Produktdesign

Interior design object made of fleece
Source: krupka–stieghan Studio für Produktdesign

RECREATE TEXTILES

The work of the Berlin design studio krupka-stieghan revolves around fibres of another kind. Together with the towel manufacturer MÖVE, the studio has developed interior design objects made of fleece and bioplastic fibres under the name "Recreate Textiles", using fluff, yarns and cut-off strands from towel production. The designers therefore put to use waste materials from the textile industry that had previously been discarded. Their products are made of textile waste from the towel manufacturer's local factory near Berlin. The combination of non-woven and natural fibre synthetic materials won through various processes along with various bioplastics means that the objects are not only bio-based but also biodegradable. The multi-coloured marbled pattern and texture that results from the materials and forming process give the recycled objects a particularly striking and attractive appearance for use in the design of interiors and furnishings.

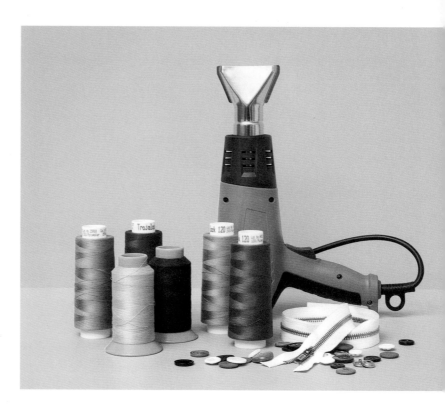

Global Change Award Winner 2018: Smart Stitch – seams that dissolve at high temperature
Source: Resortecs®

Smart Stitch simplifies the repair of clothes and the recycling of sewn-on items
Source: Cédric Vanhoeck and Vanessa Counaert/Resortecs®

SMART STITCH

The Belgian project "Smart Stitch" takes a completely different approach to combatting the increasing demand for raw materials for new fabrics. Cédric Vanhoeck, founder of Regeneration in Ghent, develops garments under the Resortecs® brand that can be easily recycled thanks to a special stitching thread produced by the company. The thread dissolves at temperatures of around 120–130 °C, much simplifying the process of recycling old clothes. Sewn-on items such as buttons, beads or zips can be removed quickly and inexpensively, and if the thread is used for stitching an entire garment, large sections of textile can simply be reused for new garments or alternatively easily be replaced when worn.

Concrete cylinder made of
organic concrete
Source: Federal Institute for
Materials Research and Testing

Acacia gum
Source: Federal Institute for
Materials Research and Testing

Sugar cane ash
Source: Federal Institute for
Materials Research and Testing

NATURAL AGGREGATES

Cassava root
Source: Federal Institute for
Materials Research and Testing

Recent new developments in the field of concrete manufacturing are exploring the use of agricultural waste in the production of building materials as a means not just of using primary materials but also of reducing carbon dioxide emissions. For years, the construction industry has been one of the main producers of carbon dioxide, and the production of concrete in particular requires large amounts of energy: the manufacture of cement clinker requires high temperatures and the curing process also involves high carbon dioxide emissions. Experts estimate that the cement industry is responsible for around 8 % of global carbon dioxide emissions.

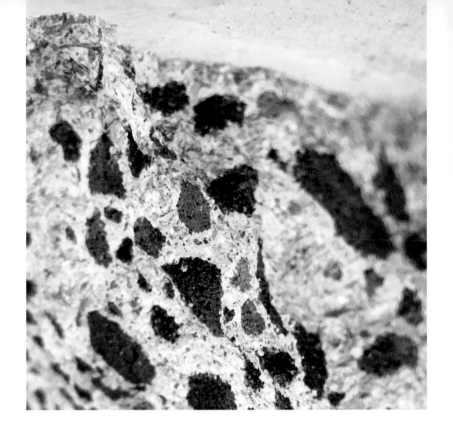

Deton – vegetable fibres
largely replace cement's
adhesive function
Source: Deton 3D Berlin

BIO-CONCRETE WITH ADDED AGRICULTURAL RESIDUES

The Federal Institute for Materials Research and Testing BAM in Berlin has developed a concrete using bio-based waste materials with a significantly reduced cement clinker content. The research team led by Dr Wolfram Schmidt drew on the experience of scientists from the University of Nigeria, using for example the highly adhesive starch of the skin of the cassava root as an additive. In Nigeria, the starchy root plant is one of the most important foodstuffs. Ash from the burnt skins of the root contain a high proportion of reactive silicon dioxide and can serve as a sustainable cement substitute, thereby improving the concrete's ecological balance. Other ingredients in the concrete formulation include coconut fibre, acacia gum, rice husks and sugar cane ash.

DETON

Nail Förderer pursues a similar approach with his concrete composite material Deton 3D. For its production, he employs vegetable fibres to largely replace the cement's adhesive function, making it possible to significantly reduce the cement content compared to normal concrete. The specific concrete formulation also obviates the need for additional waterproofing, fire protection agents or fungicides. The additional reinforcement provided by the vegetable fibres even makes it unnecessary to use steel reinforcement. In combination with foamed glass as an aggregate, Deton concrete also has very good thermal insulation properties.

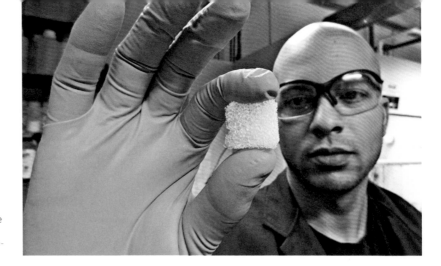

Self-destructing foam made
of liquid lignin
Source: Center for Sustainable Polymers, University of Minnesota

CHEMICAL RECYCLING

Recyclable elastomers
Source: Marc Hillmyer, Valerian
Materials

Marc Hillmyer and his team at the Department of Sustainable Polymers at the University of Minnesota have developed an environmentally friendly plastic that decomposes
back into its raw materials after use. Under normal conditions the polymers remain
stable, but when heated or exposed to a specific light source, the molecular chains
disintegrate into their individual parts. The chemically recycled raw materials can then
be recombined to form new, high-quality polymers.

The scientists compare the principle of chemical recycling with a zip: in the production
of regular petroleum-based plastics, the individual molecules are excited in such a
way that they interlock to form long molecule chains. This compound remains permanently stable and can no longer be dissolved. The plastics Hillmyer has produced in
the laboratory, by contrast, are made for example with lignin, a substance that naturally consists of individual molecules and does not form polymers. Only in combination with certain admixtures do they form molecular chains and remain stable under
normal conditions. To separate the compound like a zip, one of the components must
be stimulated by a specific impulse such as heat or light. For example, the chemists
developed a foam that decomposes at temperatures of around 200 °C. The individual
molecules are obtained with the help of bacteria from maize plants or beets.

In terms of its technical properties, the biofoam is just as performant as petrochemical foams and can be used as a packaging and cushioning material. If manufacturers
were to commit themselves to taking back products such as couch suites or car seats,
chemical recycling could be a feasible option despite its current high cost. Hillmyer
and his team have now founded a company called Valerian Materials, which offers not
only foams but also elastomers that can be chemically recycled.

Cellulose is the most ab-
undant structural molecule in
the world. Microscope image
of cellulose fibres from oats
Source: Fraunhofer IMWS

CELLULOSE-BASED MATERIALS

Wood-chip waste from
forestry
Source: Grünkunft

Cellulose is found in the cell walls of almost all plants. As one of the most important organic compounds in the world, it is used in various industries and is regarded
among scientists as a serious alternative to petroleum-based raw materials. Cellulose is won industrially from wood together with lignin and sugar and used for the
production of insulating materials, for paper and textile production as well as in the
food industry to stabilise the mixture of fruit pulp and water in orange juice. When
obtained from the waste material of cellulose-rich wood, the renewable raw material
can be considered particularly sustainable. Branches, tree parts with growth impuri-
ties, bushes or recycled wood that is of no use to the construction or furniture industry
can all be used to produce cellulose.

Paperbricks made of recycled
newspaper
Source: studio woojai

COMPOSTABLE WOOD CELLULOSE PACKAGING

Edna and Christoph Kleber run "Grünkunft", the world's first supermarket without plastic packaging. In their shop in Wasserburg am Inn in southern Germany they sell cereals, muesli and other dry goods in sustainable bags that they call "Nachhältern", a name that combines the German words for sustainability and receptacle. Made not of plastic but of 100 % cellulose from renewable sources, the packaging can be disposed of as regular waste paper or on the household compost heap. The bags are sealed with a sown paper yarn. The tear-resistant and tasteless packaging film is produced from forestry offcut waste using a viscose process and its transparency is a product of mechanical processing without chemical additives. Although the film is water-soluble, it is stable enough to safely transport the contents back home even when exposed to heavy rain for several minutes.

Compostable packaging
made of 100 % cellulose
Source: Grünkunft

PAPERBRICKS

Paper can be recycled, but not without a decline in quality. With each cycle, the fibres grow shorter reducing their stability. After five to seven cycles, the fibres are no longer usable for paper production. The Korean designer WooJai Lee uses recycled paper that is no longer recyclable to make modular connecting elements for furniture and other interior design objects. He shreds old newspapers, mixes the paper flakes with wood glue and allows the mixture to harden into predefined shapes. After drying, the material can be worked using traditional woodworking techniques such as sawing, sanding and milling. His "Paperbricks" are a remarkably robust upcycling product and are not only strong and stable but also express the qualities of the raw material through their velvety surface texture.

Cellulose cartilage material
from old jeans
Source: Donna Squire/deakin

ARTIFICIAL CARTILAGE MADE FROM
RECYCLED DENIM FABRIC

Scientists at Deakin University in Melbourne have developed a biocompatible material made from recycled cellulose fibres that can in future be used to make custom-produced cartilage implants for patients using a 3D printer. The cellulose molecule is extracted from old jeans by dissolving them in liquid solvents. The resulting material can then be used to produce a cellulose-based aerogel that has similar qualities to animal cartilage. Although cellulose aerogels already exist on the market, what sets this apart is the process of upcycling waste material from other sectors such as discarded clothing for use as high-quality medical components in joint reconstruction.

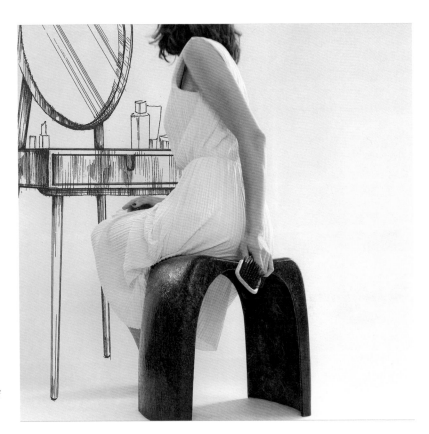

Dressing table stool made of human hair
Source: Oksana Bondar

ANIMAL MATERIALS

Human hair – an uncommon raw material direct from the hairdresser
Source: Haute Innovation

Whether in household organic waste or at the hairdresser's, young designers in search of untapped sources of raw materials close to home have discovered valuable human and animal waste and transformed them into sustainable and aesthetic everyday objects using traditional craft techniques such as felting.

STOOL MADE OF HUMAN HAIR

With her "Wiggy Stool", the designer Oksana Bondar demonstrates the potential of a previously unused human residue. While researching local waste streams, the London-based designer identified human hair clippings as an abundant and valuable but neglected fibre. Through material experimentation, she discovered that hair can be wet felted and formed into solid shapes by laminating it with polylactide acid (PLA) bioplastic. The result is a stool that, on account of its simplified form, not only illustrates the stability of the material but above all its aesthetics.

Tableware made of charred
vegetable waste
Source: Kosuke Araki

TABLEWARE MADE FROM ORGANIC WASTE

Kosuke Araki, a designer from Tokyo, has created an unusual range of tableware comprising cups, plates and bowls from recycled organic waste. For his "Anima Collection", he collected his own organic waste, separating it into animal and plant matter. After two years, he had amassed a good 315 kg of leftover food, bones, egg and vegetable bowls. In order to transform the organic waste into a new material, Araki first burned the plant matter into coal and then pulverized it. He boiled the animal matter, including bones and skin, to extract glue from it. After shaping and drying the finished objects, he sealed their surfaces with urushi, a natural varnish that has been widely used in Japan for centuries.

Pigments from human hair
Source: Leopold Seiler

INK FROM HAIR

As part of the "reuse" semester studio at Burg Giebichenstein in Halle, Leopold Seiler likewise investigated the possibilities offered by hair. His project "Your hair – Your ink" examines the unique quality of the material. Working together with the biochemical laboratory at Martin Luther University, he gently dissolved various different samples of hair enzymatically to obtain pigments, which were then used to make personally unique inks.

The mixing proportions determine the colour of the tiles
Source: Lea Schücking

Tiles made from recycled bricks and waste glass
Source: Lea Schücking

RECYCLED BUILDING MATERIALS

In terms of quantity, construction waste such as tiles, concrete or shards of broken glass represents one of the largest sources of waste. In 2014, some 54.6 million t of construction waste were produced in Germany alone. Although around four fifths of this is recycled and a further portion is used as ballast for road construction, the amount that ends up in landfill sites each year still stretches available capacities. Reason enough then for developers, architects and designers to tackle the problem and explore new ideas for materials and closed material cycles.

TILES MADE FROM BUILDING RUBBLE

The young designer Lea Schücking from Kassel has created a series of tiles made from building rubble under the name "Shards" that have an unusual surface structure and haptic qualities. Each tile is unique. She crushes brick rubble and waste glass into a granulate that she mixes, forms and fires into new tiles. By varying the mixing proportions and firing temperature, the colouring can be adjusted from bright green to brown tones without needing additional pigments. Her idea creates a circular system in which waste material from building rubble is converted into a high-quality product without compromising material quality or consuming large amounts of energy.

Tom van Soest and Ward
Massa from StoneCycling
Source: StoneCycling

The brick production process
uses 25 % less energy than
traditional processes
Source: StoneCycling

STONECYCLING

Demolishing buildings produces a considerable amount of different materials. For the designer Tom van Soest, these waste materials serve as a basis for new building materials and were the starting point for a business idea. Together with Ward Massa, he founded StoneCycling in 2013, which makes building materials from recycled building rubble. During his studies in Eindhoven, the young Dutchman had already experimented with transforming different waste materials into new building materials. After much experimentation, he found ways in which to create new building materials from old glass windows, bricks, tiles, concrete debris and even old toilet bowls. The waste is collected and pre-sorted into material groups before being crushed and ground into fine powder. Depending on the desired strength and appearance, the designers blend the various constituents and melt them together to form a solid brick or small-format slab. The exact recipe of the new product mixtures is a closely guarded secret. According to the designers, the brick production process requires no binding chemicals and uses 25 % less energy than traditional processes. A number of building projects using their waste-based bricks have already been built in the Netherlands, Luxembourg, England and Belgium.

34 % of beverage cartons were recycled in Europe in 2014

Source: Ruby Odilia Photo Lab

BUILDING MATERIALS FROM PACKAGING

China's import ban on 24 different recycling materials came into force on 1 January 2018 in response to the vast quantities of plastic, textile and waste paper shipped to China from Europe. The ban also stopped the import, processing and disposal of unsorted plastic waste from the USA and Japan. Until then, plastic waste was either sorted manually, a time-consuming process, or incinerated in partly outdated waste incineration plants. China's decision to end this practice is also a product of its intention to develop its own circular economies. Environmentalists view this development optimistically, as it indirectly places the onus on the exporting industrialised nations to implement more efficient recycling strategies for the various types of plastics and to reuse raw materials.

Over nine billion beverage cartons are sold every year in Germany alone. They are lightweight, not subject to a returns deposit and frequently also reclosable thanks to a screw cap. Most beverage cartons consist of three different materials combined into a composite container: an aluminium and plastic lining made of polyethylene (PE) to optimally protect the liquid contents from light and oxygen, and a stabilising cardboard enclosure. The manufacturers claim a recycling rate of 70 %: the valuable cellulose fibres of the cardboard box are processed by paper mills into cardboard or corrugated board, while the remaining, virtually inseparable plastic–aluminium foil ends up in the furnaces of cement works, where it is used as a substitute for the aluminium ore bauxite.

As an alternative to incineration, packaging materials could be separated by type and returned directly to the respective material cycles or converted directly into products and building materials. A number of new developments have emerged in recent years to explore these options.

Furniture made from recycled
beverage cartons
Source: ETH Zurich / Professor Dirk
Hebel

WASTE VAULT PAVILION

For the IDEAS City Festival in New York in May 2015, Dirk Hebel's team from the ETH Zurich and Philippe Block's research group built a 90 m² pavilion of recycled beverage cartons. In order to transform them into a useful building material, they were first shredded and then pressed into boards with the addition of heat. The plastic coating on the outside and inside of the carton acts as an adhesive. The curved roof canopy demonstrates the potential of sustainable building materials based on packaging waste for temporary construction projects. Given the need to decarbonise the construction industry, the recycled composite material represents a sustainable alternative to traditional concrete construction as it not only presents a way of recycling material waste but also reduces the energy required for construction.

One brick made of 20 PET bottles
Source: Leonard Te Laak / Studio Köster

Insulating building material made from PET bottles
Source: Fundación Ecoinclusión Alta Gracia, Córdoba

BRIDGE MADE OF RECYCLED PLASTIC

In 2011, the first recycled plastic bridge in Europe was installed over the River Tweed in Easter Dawyck, about 50 km south of Edinburgh. With a span of almost 30 m and a loadbearing capacity of 44 t, it is the longest roadway bridge made of recycled plastic in the world. The individual sections of the bridge were manufactured in the USA from approximately 50 t of recycled polyethylene and assembled in Scotland. In contrast to bridges made of wood or steel, the plastic bridge does not rust or suffer from insect infestation, keeping maintenance to a minimum. In addition, the plastic structural elements require neither complex and costly surface finishings nor coatings to protect them against the weather.

BRICKS MADE OF PLASTIC BOTTLES

In Argentina, 12 million PET bottles are thrown away every day. Only 1.8 million of them – a mere 15 % – are actually recycled. The non-profit organisation Fundación Ecoinclusión uses PET bottles to produce bricks and other building materials. According to the three founders, Fabian Saieg, Leandro Lima and Leandro Miguez, a 1.5 kg brick can be made from around 20 plastic bottles, which are shredded into PET flakes and mixed with cement. The mixture is compressed into bricks under high pressure. The company donates the loadbearing and insulating recycling bricks for the construction of publicly subsidised social housing.

Durable road surface with 100 %-recycled plastic additives
Source: Leonard Te Laak / Studio Köster

ROAD SURFACE MADE FROM HARD-TO-RECYCLE PLASTIC

The Scottish company MacRebur has developed a new type of road surface. Using a specially developed process, plastic waste is first converted into pellets, that are added to the asphalt mix and act as a binding agent much like petroleum-based bitumen. The plastic content can amount to up to 20 % of the mass of the road surface. PET or other plastics that are easy to recycle are not used; only plastics that would otherwise be sent for incineration. By adjusting the mixing ratio, a quiet rolling surface can be produced, which is ideal for use in areas where traffic noise is an issue such as residential areas. The road surfacing is also harder and more durable than conventional asphalt, substantially reducing the need for repair and maintenance. According to MacRebur, the company has already built roads in over 50 countries on all continents of the world.

Countless pieces of old chewing gum are scratched off
pavements every year
Source: Haute Innovation

110,000 m³ of autumn leaves
accumulate every year in
Berlin alone
Source: Ruby Odilia Photo Lab

37 % of all smoked cigarettes
are thrown on the ground
Source: Haute Innovation

URBAN WASTE

The term urban mining has emerged in recent years in conjunction with the recycling
of valuable metals and other secondary raw materials from the city. Urban dwellers are
no longer just consumers but also producers of valuable resources. Although Europe is
not rich in resources, there are enough recyclable materials that can be fed back into
circular material cycles. Aside from traditional recycling materials such as glass, paper
or plastic, unusual waste materials such as leaves and coffee grounds are increasingly
being used to produce new products. Even old chewing gum and cigarette ends recovered from pavements have potential to be recycled.

Beleaf Chair
Source: Šimon Kern

The British start-up bio-bean produces biofuel from coffee grounds
Source: bio-bean

Beleaf Chair
Source: Šimon Kern

BELEAF CHAIR

Every autumn, roads and pavements are cleared of leaves to avoid accidents resulting from people or vehicles slipping on wet leaves. In Berlin alone, as much as 110,000 m³ of leaves are swept from the streets in the autumn months. The organic matter is processed in large composting plants into nutrient-rich compost. The Slovakian designer Šimon Kern has found other uses for leaves and employs them as a material in his designs for chairs and lamps. By mixing dried leaves with a bio-resin made from frying oils, he has created a compostable seat which he calls the Beleaf Chair.

BIODIESEL FROM COFFEE GROUNDS

Some of the 9,500 buses on London's roads already run on fuels made from waste products such as cooking oil and tallow from meat processing. Working in collaboration with Shell, the start-up bio-beans has identified another urban waste product suitable for fuel production: coffee grounds. The oil in coffee grounds is extracted and added to diesel fuel. Up to 20% of this new biodiesel is comprised of coffee oil. To ensure an adequate and consistent supply of coffee grounds, the British company cooperates with large coffee consumers such as canteens, cafés and restaurants, who collect the valuable resource instead of discarding it. So far, only the coffee's aroma has been used, while the remaining 99% of the grounds are discarded unused.

99 % of ground coffee beans
are discared unused
Source: Ruby Odilia Photo Lab

Frayed cigarette filters made
of cellulose acetate
Source: Haute Innovation

PARK BENCHES MADE FROM USED CIGARETTE FILTERS

According to a study in the medical journal "The Lancet" from 2017, there are currently 933 million smokers in the world. Although information campaigns on the health risks of smoking have led to a decline in the percentage of smokers around the world, the increasing global population has led to a rise in the number of smokers in absolute terms compared with 1990. According to TerraCycle from New Jersey, on average 37 % of all smoked cigarettes are carelessly thrown on the ground. This is both an aesthetic as well as an ecological problem, because the cellulose acetate fibres of the filter are not biodegradable. TerraCycle separates the filters from the organic components such as ash, tobacco and paper and converts them using a thermal process into products as diverse as park benches and transport pallets. The company has installed ashtrays on street lamps in cities throughout the United States and Canada and empties them free of charge as a service to the cities. Individuals can also download free shipping labels from the recycler's website to send in their own collected cigarette ends. Since the programme was launched in 2012, more than 90 million cigarette ends have been collected at over 12,000 locations in North America and Australia.

The average pavement in Germany has up to 80 discarded chewing gums per square metre
Source: Ruby Odilia Photo Lab

The first sneaker in the world made of recycled chewing gum
Source: Ruby Odilia Photo Lab

GUMSHOE

In many cities, chewing gum is just as much a nuisance as cigarette ends. In the Netherlands, more than 1.5 million kg of chewing gum are scraped from roads and pavements every year. Together with the recycling company Gumdrop Ltd from London, the marketing department of the city of Amsterdam has presented a sneaker with an outer sole made entirely of recycled old chewing gum. For the first 500 pairs of GumShoes, 250 kg of chewing gum mass were melted and moulded to make the outer soles.

Urban furniture made of
plastic waste
Source: Print Your City

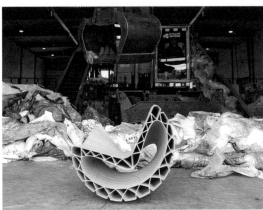

Europeans produce more
than 30 kg of plastic waste
per head each year
Source: Print Your City

PRINT YOUR CITY

The Rotterdam-based design studio "The New Raw" is turning plastic waste into street furniture for public spaces. The architects Foteini Setaki and Panos Sakkas use a 3D printer with a robot arm to produce objects made of recycled plastic for public spaces. With their project, the designers aim to draw attention to the problem of increasing plastic waste. The initial prototype for the project is the 1.5-m-long "XXX bench" 3D-printed from 50 kg of recycled plastic. The street furniture is produced by Aectual, a company near Amsterdam that can produce large format items using a giant granulate printer with a robot arm.

BIOECONOMICS AND BIO-BASED MATERIALS

Mushrooms – a novel material for the future
Source : Haute Innovation

The summer of 2018 in Central and Northern Europe was exceptionally dry, leading to water shortages that are uncommon in these latitudes. The extremely hot summer and subsequent dry autumn caused economic losses running into the tens of billions. Crop failures, parched parks in cities, forest fires, interruptions to shipping transport and the resulting supply bottlenecks for numerous industries have caused costly long-term damage to the economy and society. Experts from the Center for Disaster Management and Risk Reduction Technology (CEDIM) at Karlsruhe Institute of Technology (KIT) predict that the effects of the historic drought will continue to be felt in the coming years. In addition, scientists expect such extreme weather conditions to continue in future. Although meteorologists point out that it is not unusual for extreme weather fluctuations and natural disasters such as droughts and floods to occur at irregular intervals, it becomes more critical when the intervals between these extremes become shorter and more regular. Scientists and researchers around the world attribute this worrying development to climate change and are calling for urgent action to halt the trend of global warming.

With the successful ratification of the internationally binding climate treaty in Paris on 12 December 2015, all 196 states spoke out in favour of limiting the rise in global average temperature to well below 2 °C above its pre-industrial level. To limit the risks and effects of climate change, however, the temperature increase should be closer to 1.5 °C if possible. This ambitious goal can only be achieved by making drastic energy

Algae as an alternative raw material
Source: Haute Innovation

Textiles made of mushroom-based material
Source: Diana Drewes

Tuesa storage containers protect food from spoiling
Source: Anastasiya Koshcheeva

savings and limiting CO_2 emissions considerably. In this context, recent research initiatives have increasingly focused on material innovations based on renewable raw materials, as the CO_2 balance for production and disposal is much lower compared with other energy-intensive materials. Many countries have declared it their political intention to shift their economies away from dependency on fossil fuels and raw materials towards other sustainable and locally available alternatives.

In the search for alternative natural and sustainable raw materials, young designers in particular are now rediscovering unusual and in some cases long-overlooked sources and are using intelligent design to transform traditional crafts and techniques into skills for creating innovative products. Numerous projects examine ways of using biomass and previously neglected waste and by-product materials. Pineapple fibres, coffee grounds or algae are being used to produce robust textiles, dandelion rubber is being tapped as a new resource for car tyres, and microorganisms are being employed for the production of building materials. By establishing new value chains for locally available biomass, we are practising the sustainable and efficient use of resources, as nature has always done, and paving the way towards a climate-neutral economy.

Interior design object made
of propolis
Source: Marlène Huissoud

BIO-BASED RESINS

With the rising awareness among many young designers of their ability to positively influence future consumer behaviour through their choice of ecologically friendly materials, focus has begun to shift back towards long-overlooked natural materials and their respective crafts and techniques. Aside from the use of natural fibres, natural adhesives such as a bio-based resins now play an important role in the new designs and concepts of up-and-coming young designers.

PROPOLIS

Propolis is a natural resin with a brownish to black colour that is produced by bees to seal cells in the hive. It consists of thickened plant juices, solids such as pollen and various essential oils that make it resistant to bacteria and fungi. The French designer Marlène Huissoud uses the techniques of glass production to shape the natural thermoplastic material. As part of her project "From Insects", she has created vessels and smaller interior design objects.

Wooden Leather using the
silk protein sericin
Source: Marlène Huissoud

Birch tar
Source: Paul Kozowyk

WOODEN LEATHER

Inspired by the smart properties of animal-produced materials, Marlène Huissoud discovered the silk protein sericin in the secretions of silkworms and the binding effect it has under the influence of water and heat. In combination with heated, fluid propolis, the fine silk fibre mesh can be pressed into a hard and resistant composite material.

BIRCH TAR

Birch tar is a pitch-black and tar-like substance extracted from birch bark. It is considered the oldest adhesive in the world and was used as far back as prehistoric times for making tools and weapons. The waterproof glue is produced by burning birch bark using so-called dry distillation. Birch tar behaves like other natural resins and can therefore be classified as a hot-melt adhesive (HMA). Bonded items can therefore be detached by heating.

Breeding high-yield
dandelion plants
Source: Continental

Taraxagum – car tyres made
using dandelion rubber
Source: Continental

BIO-BASED ELASTOMERS

Many everyday products such as car tyres, balloons or condoms are made of natural rubber or latex, the milky sap of the rubber tree. The mass-processing of this special raw material began in the early 19th century and made Brazil an enormously wealthy country. Although the rubber tree now thrives in the tropical climates of Southeast Asia, India and West Africa, the existing plantations cannot meet rising global demand. Researchers from all over the world are now rediscovering previously forgotten rubber substitutes and developing new, competitive alternatives.

DANDELION RUBBER

Together with the Fraunhofer Institute for Molecular Biology and Applied Ecology (IME), the tyre manufacturer Continental has developed a manufacturing process for the production of natural rubber from dandelion juice. A Russian species of dandelion has proven to be particularly rich in rubber. After centrifuging the dandelion milk, the pure rubber can be skimmed off the surface. In recent years, Continental has worked on optimising the breeding process and developing the corresponding production technology and has now begun working on ways of mass-producing the material. To this end, a 30,000 m² research and testing laboratory was opened at the end of 2018 in Anklam in northeast Germany, in the state of Mecklenburg-Western Pomerania.

Grass used as an additive
for latex
Soucre: Haute Innovation

GRASS CONDOMS

Researchers at Queensland University in Australia use grass from the outback to make latex products such as condoms and rubber gloves both thinner and more resilient. Using a combination of mechanical and chemical processes, they extract nanocellulose from spinifex, a species of grass indigenous to the arid regions of Australia, and use this as an additive for conventional latex. The small cellulose fibrils and crystals have excellent properties. They are already used as implants in medical technology and as a reinforcing agent in combination with latex.

Foam made with the addition
of soybean oil
Source: F. Anwarowna Chamitowa

BIO-BASED FOAMS

Bio-based foams are used in the automotive, furniture and construction industries. They are also familiar to many as a packaging material for fragile freight. Foams are useful due to their low weight, their insulating effect and their elastic properties. However, industrially produced foams are currently the product of petrochemical process chains. The first step towards bio-based alternatives was achieved by partially replacing some petroleum-based components with natural polymers. To make completely bio-based foams, however, the entire process has to be changed.

SOY FOAM

Several years ago, Ford presented a soy foam that has since been used in the car manufacturer's car seats. Although the upholstery material does not consist entirely of the renewable raw material, by adding soy oil it has been possible to reduce the proportion of crude oil to 60 %.

ALGAE-BASED ETHYLENE-VINYL ACETATE COPOLYMER (EVA) FOAM

The US company Bloom has developed an EVA foam that consists of up to 60 % algae. According to the manufacturer, this proportion represents a safe value for reliably producing the open-cell expanded mix of synthetic and natural rubber. As with all integral foams, the inside forms a sponge-like structure while the outer skin is dense and thus waterproof. The foam is already being used in Vivobarefoot outdoor shoes.

Packaging made of wood
foam
Source: Fraunhofer WKI

Wood foam made of ligno-
cellulose
Source: Fraunhofer WKI

WOOD FOAM

The Fraunhofer Institute for Wood Research Wilhelm-Klauditz-Institut (WKI) in Braunschweig has developed a process for the production of pressure-resistant foams out of lignocellulose. Both hardwood and softwood are used as raw materials. The strength of the wood foam is a product of the wood's own binding forces, and the foams therefore consist of 100 % renewable raw materials. The process is also suitable for lignocellulose from non-wood materials such as hemp or straw. The researchers have succeeded not only in developing a compostable and lightweight construction material but also in producing a wide range of rigid foam boards as well as elastic foams for packaging and insulation applications.

Milk with vinegar
Source: Haute Innovation

CASEIN PLASTICS

Containers made of casein plastics
Source: Tessa Silva Dawson

Strict food laws in many countries and food overproduction have provided the impetus for researchers and designers to rediscover the oldest plastic in the world and its unusual properties. The formula for the production of casein plastic was developed in Bavaria back in 1530. At that time, it was already clear that whey formed during the acidification of milk and that in the process white flakes were deposited on the surface. This so-called casein can be skimmed off and is malleable while still warm and wet. As it dries, the natural polymer hardens to form a solid material. In industrial production, dried casein powder is produced from whey, which is mixed with water or other liquids depending on the desired product properties.

Edible plastic granulate from casein
Source: Lactips

Milk that is not suitable for sale can be used to make plastic
Source: Tessa Silva Dawson

PROTEIN

In her "Protein" project, the young designer Tessa Silva Dawson returns to the original recipe and shows that the production of casein plastic does not require a complex chemical synthesis process. Rather than obtaining her raw material from the super-market, the designer sources milk that dairies are unable to use due to strict food regulations, for example from sick or calving cows. Similarly, centrifuged milk from cheese production is likewise surplus to requirements but can be used for the production of casein plastic.

EDIBLE MILK PACKAGING

The French company Lactips has developed an edible packaging film for food that is made of casein. According to the scientists, the casein film significantly increases the shelf life of the packaged food and can even be consumed afterwards. The first applications of the water-soluble film have been for bags of rice and portioned dry goods such as cornflakes or wine gums. The raw material is a mixture of commercially available casein powder and water, which is first poured to form thermoplastic granules and then formed into an extremely thin film.

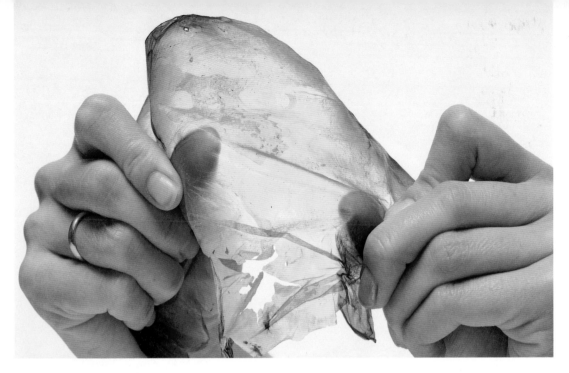

Cultivated textile made of
fungal mycelium
Source: Haute Innovation

MUSHROOM-BASED
MATERIALS

Mycelium as a binder
Source: Haute Innovation

Mushrooms have taken on a new meaning for designers and material developers in
recent years. The company Ecovative Design in New York has played a particular role in
generating renewed interest in considering the potential of fungi not just as a means
of decomposition but as a tool for composition. They developed a mushroom-bonded
packaging material that is made from agricultural industrial waste and fine mushroom
fibres that normally form networks underground. The combination of fungal mycelium
and vegetable waste results in a completely compostable material that has a feel,
weight and appearance reminiscent of polystyrene. Inspired and impressed by the
rapid growth and versatile applications of mushrooms, numerous new products have
emerged that are already in use today in products for end consumers.

Textiles made of mushroom-
based material
Source: MycoWorks

Bodysurfing handplane
with mushroom mycelium-
bonded foam core
Source: Ecovative Design

MYCO SURFBOARD

In cooperation with Ecovative Design, a Californian sports equipment manufacturer has brought out the first surfboard with a mushroom foam core. By not using petroleum-based foams, they are demonstratively taking a stand against the littering of the world's oceans. Although the outer shell is still stabilised with resilient synthetic resins, the overall product makes a valuable contribution. According to the manufacturers, numerous broken or forgotten surfboards are left behind on beaches and get drawn out to sea every year.

MUSHROOM-BASED TEXTILES

Experts are not the only people to prize the reishi mushroom as an elastic and uncomplicated mushroom. The mycelium filaments that form remain highly elastic, even after drying, and thus offer greater potential for use than other, often brittle fungal species. The founders of MycoWorks have exploited this quality for their fungus-based textiles. To make larger surfaces more flexible, as well as to alter the colour or haptic feel, the fungal material is combined with different cellulose-like plant fibres. Since the mycelium threads are microscopically small, it is possible to grow different material thicknesses.

Antibacterial handles made
of birch bark
Source: Betula Manus

BARK MATERIALS

Bark is the "skin" of trees. It protects the tree from wind and weather and infestation by microorganisms. Each species of tree stores different secondary plant substances in the bark such as betulin, essential oils or tanning agents. Under the outer bark is a layer of air-filled, dead cells, commonly known as cork. Depending on the tree, this hard, foam-like layer can be several centimetres thick. In the wood-processing industry, some four million cubic metres of tree bark accumulate annually as a by-product in Germany alone. It is frequently used to make adhesives or tanning extracts. In other parts of the world, tree bark is peeled directly from the tree up to twice a year and processed for use as bottle corks, textile substitutes, floor coverings or insulation boards.

BIRCH BARK

Up to 30 % of birch bark consists of betulin. The secondary plant substance gives the tree its white colour and protects it from UV radiation. It also gives the bark antimycotic and antibacterial properties. Birch bark has long been valued for its high durability, mechanical tear resistance, good breathability, water-repellence and specific haptic quality and was used widely, especially in Russian, Scandinavian and Canadian crafts. However, as it was more difficult to process industrially, it has been almost entirely displaced by modern plastics and the market practically disappeared. That has now changed with the advent of the Betula Manus brand, and the material is currently

Chair and ottoman combination with seat and backrest made of birch bark
Source: Anastasiya Koshcheeva

Taburet stool made of anti-bacterial birch bark strips
Source: Anastasiya Koshcheeva

experiencing a renaissance. New technical methods have since made it possible to bond and industrially process the material. Through its combination of hydrophobic and antibacterial properties, it has numerous potential applications. Whether used as a floor covering in wet rooms, for door handles in day care centres or push buttons in elevators or trains, the antibacterial properties of birch bark are potentially beneficial in many heavily frequented places.

FURNITURE DESIGN USING BIRCH BARK

The Russian designer Anastasiya Koshcheeva has developed a novel concept for the use of birch bark in furniture design. Under the name "Sibirjak", she has designed an armchair and ottoman combination that uses the largest currently available sheets of birch bark stretched over its frame. The horizontal alignment of the bark underlines the leather-like properties of the material and creates an inviting, generous seating surface. The seat of her "Taburet" stool takes another approach, weaving strips of birch bark into a three-dimensional striped mesh.

Tuesa storage containers
protect food from spoiling
Source: Anastasiya Koshcheeva

Tuesa storage container
made of antibacterial birch
bark
Source: Anastasiya Koshcheeva

TUESA STORAGE CONTAINER

Due to its antibacterial properties, birch bark is ideal for storing food. The material of the "Tuesa" storage containers hinders mould formation and significantly extends the shelf life of its contents. Oatmeal biscuits, for example, remain fresh and crunchy in the containers for two weeks.

TANNIN

Tannin is found in grapes or in the bark of acacia, oak, chestnut and other trees rich in tanning agents. Researchers and scientists use it to produce adhesives for building materials such as chipboard and MDF. Physicians at Korea Advanced Institute of Science and Technology (KAIST) in South Korea are also exploring a new application for use in surgery: a special wet plaster to prevent internal bleeding. According to the scientists, the addition of tannin doubles the adhesive strength of conventional fibrin plasters made of biocompatible polyethylene glycol.

Bag and shoes made of Pinatex
Source: Ananas Anam

VEGETABLE LEATHER SUBSTITUTE

Pineapple leaf fibres
Source: Ananas Anam

Shopping for shoes is particularly challenging for animal lovers and committed vegans because of the lack of alternatives to animal leather. Synthetically produced upper materials are also ecologically problematic due to their use of petrochemical raw materials. This has not escaped the attention of designers and fans of old craft techniques. In recent years, they have developed innovative textiles that exhibit the robustness of leather, but are of vegetable origin.

PINATEX

Ananas Anam, based in London, sells a leather substitute made from the fibres of pineapple leaves. The idea originates from the Philippines, where for generations a leather-like fabric called "Barong Talong" has been made out of the resistant and durable plant fibres. The company's founder Carmen Hijosa discovered the traditional craft in the 1990s and has since optimised it to such an extent that it now represents a serious alternative to conventional animal leather in the fashion industry. The results of the first cooperative projects with bag designers and shoe manufacturers are already on the market.

FRUITLEATHER

In the Netherlands, the designers Koen Meerkerk and Hugo de Boon have also found value in food waste materials. They use not only the fibres of apple, pear or mango skins, but also the pectin that the skins contain. Pectin is a cold-setting, natural gelling agent. Although numerous recipes for the production of fruit leather can be found online, the two designers keep their own recipe closely guarded and have not revealed whether they add waxes or oils to keep the leather durable. In any case, the material represents a sustainable alternative for fast fashion products such as bags.

ORANGE LEATHER

A replacement for leather made of orange peel
Source: Elise Esser

In the "Innovative Product Design" course at Niederrhein University of Applied Sciences, Elise Esser also examined new biodegradable textiles, in this case based on orange peel. For her newly developed material, she mixes small amounts of the polysaccharide alginate, which is obtained from red algae, with orange peel fibres. The gentle, low-chemical process she uses for the organic materials retains the bright colour pigment of the fruit peel as well as its pleasantly fragrant essential oils.

AMADOU

Hat made of Amadou
Source: Haute Innovation

Amadou looks and feels like suede. It is a soft, thick textile with a texture reminiscent of felt. The material is made of tinder fungus, a tree fungus that grows mainly on birch trees. Under the hard outer surface lies a soft spongy core called the trama. This is carefully removed from the outer shell and cooked until soft. The material which is like hard foam can then be beaten to form a large flexible surface. The tinder fungus is a parasite and absorbs betulin from the tree bark, giving the resulting spongy core antibacterial and antifungal properties. The airy structure of the dead tissue is also water-resistant. Amadou has been used as a material in Siberia for centuries and is still a popular material used for making hats, bags and vests.

NOANI

"Noani" stands for "No Animal" and is a start-up committed to fair working conditions and sustainability. Its manager Fabian Stadler sees his responsibility in the choice of raw materials, and his leather substitute – a mix of 80% eucalyptus fibres and 20% recycled PET – is made in Germany.

An alternative to leather made of fruit waste
Source: Fruitleather

Bag and shoe made of orange leather
Source: Elise Esser

Belt made of Noani material
Source: noanifashion

Amadou is as soft as silk
Source: Nina Fabert

Sneakers made using coffee grounds
Source: Sebastian Thies

COFFEE GROUNDS SNEAKERS

Sebastian Thies, a young shoemaker from Munich, is taking on the big sports shoe manufacturers with his label Nat-2, which features attractive, contemporary sneaker designs and uses innovative materials. No material is too unusual for the shoemaker: his shoe designs are made of wood, slate or antibacterial mushroom leather made from tinder fungus. A particularly unusual variant is a shoe made of coffee grounds, a readily available waste product that can easily be collected, especially in urban areas where there are many cafés. For his Nat-2 Coffee Line, the young shoemaker uses not only the coffee grounds, but also the fibres of the coffee plant. The result is a high-quality shimmering brown surface that even smells of coffee.

Grass paper
Source: Creapapier

GRASS PAPER
AND TEXTILES

Grass can be used in place of wood to make paper
Source: Haute Innovation

Paper making has followed the same basic principle for many decades. The main component is wood fibres converted into pulp in a mechanical and chemical process. The result is a thick mass, to which additives such as glue and bleaching agent are added, depending on the type of paper required. Nowadays, fresh cellulose represents only a small fraction of the pulp mix. Waste paper has since become an important raw material source in the paper industry, however recycled paper can only be reused to a limited extent. With each new cycle, the fibres shorten and can no longer mat into a stable web of fibres. In the search for alternatives for the paper industry, entrepreneurs have discovered some unusual resources. And these can also be used for textiles.

GRASS PAPER

"Creapapier" from Hennef in Germany uses grass as an alternative fibre material along with supplementary raw material for pulp or wood pulp. What sets grass apart is that it grows quickly and does not require subsequent chemical processing. In the age of paper recycling, a certain amount of fresh cellulose must be added, especially to high-quality paper grades. Coniferous softwoods such as spruce, fir or pine are best suited for the production of cellulose because their fibres are significantly longer and provide the necessary strength in combination with the usually very short and brittle recycled fibres recovered from waste paper. As grass fibres contain only a small proportion of lignin, they do not need to be chemically processed. According to the manufacturers, the grass content of packaging board can be as much as 51 %.

Paper made from elephant
dung
Source: Haute Innovation

Elephant dung
Source: Haute Innovation

Elephants in Sri Lanka
Source: Haute Innovation

ELEPHANT DUNG PAPER

A similar approach is used in Sri Lanka. The company Maximus collects elephant dung
and makes paper from it. Over 4,000 elephants live in the wild in Sri Lanka and each
animal eats an average of 180 kg of grass per day. However, the animals find the long
fibres of grass difficult to digest and excrete them. The fibres are partially decomposed
by gastric juices during the digestive process, making them soft enough for use in
paper production. The proportion of these alternative fibres can be as much as 75 %.

Fashion made from cow dung
Source: Jalila Essaïdi

Jalila Essaïdi breaks down
cow dung into its individual
constituents
Source: Jalila Essaïdi / Mike Roelofs

FASHION FROM COW DUNG

The Dutch artist Jalila Essaïdi has developed a process at BioArtLab in Eindhoven for the production of biopaper and bioplastic from cow dung. She first separated the solid and liquid components of the dung. The solid component is the dry, digested grass, while the liquid component is a mixture of gastric juices and urea, from which she extracted certain chemicals to produce cellulose from the grass. This can then be processed into cardboard or paper. If further acidic chemicals from the cow dung are added, cellulose acetate is produced from which liquid plastic can be produced. The Swedish fashion house H&M has expressed interest in using these unusual resources for the future production of textiles.

Furniture and lighting
made from an algae-paper
composite material
Source: Jonas Edvard, Nikolaj
Steenfatt

ALGAE AND ALGAE COMPOSITES

The appearance of algae is as varied as their occurrence in nature. They can be found in almost all waters. Although an integral part of the Asian diet, algae are considered to be weeds or even a plague in Western cultures. In many respects, however, algae offer potential that qualifies them as a source of biomass and an alternative raw material to petrochemical products. The key advantages of algae are that they grow rapidly, can bind carbon dioxide in the atmosphere and do not take up agricultural land. With the increasing focus on sustainability, many designers have begun to exploit algae as a resource in their designs.

THE TERROIR PROJECT

With "The Terroir Project", the product designers Jonas Edvard and Nikolaj Steenfatt from Copenhagen have demonstrated the new development of a biocomposite made of algae from the Danish coasts and paper. After drying, the algae are chopped up and boiled down to a thick pulp, extracting sodium alginates in the process to use their gelling effect. In combination with paper, the result is a biodegradable composite material that feels similar to cork and can be processed into lampshades and chair shells. Different colours can be created by using different types of algae. The high salt content of the marine plants also reduces the flammability of the products.

Naturally decomposing
bottles made of agar-agar
Source: Ari Jónsson

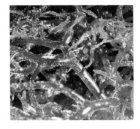

Algae as an alternative raw
material source
Source: Haute Innovation

The right material for every
form of packaging
Source: Kosuke Araki, Noriaki
Maetani & Akira Muraoka / AMAM

AGAR PLASTICITY

The design studio AMAM from Japan uses different algae to produce films and light-weight packaging material. The cell walls of red and blue algae contain so-called agar-agar, a galactose polymer that is commonly used in vegan cuisine as a vegetable gelling agent. To extract the agar-agar from the cell walls, the sun-dried algae are first boiled, the mass then dried and ground to fine powder. When dissolved in water or other liquids, it serves as a thickening agent. In extensive material tests, the design studio trialled a large number of material mixtures of agar-agar and water that in future could replace non-compostable plastic for packaging. Depending on the desired end product, not only the proportions of the individual constituents vary, but also the subsequent processing steps: For lightweight, foam-like packaging materials, for example, the material is rapidly cooled or even frozen. For film-like structures, the material must be compressed into a thin layer.

Algae textiles from fine-
fibred algae species
Source: Melanie Glöckler

MARINE COTTON

At Burg Giebichenstein in Halle, Germany, designers have been working for several years on unusual application scenarios for fast-growing algae biomass. Melanie Glöckler, for example, proposed a possible use in the textile industry with her project "Marine Cotton", which shows various techniques for using fine-fibre algae species for yarns and felt-like scrims. The different results derive from the observation that in water the fibres are loose and easy to arrange, but once exposed to air they begin to dry, forming a sticky and stable bond.

AL G. textile made of
algae-based yarn
Source: Juni Sun Neyenhuys

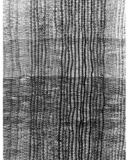

AL G. – TRANSFORMATION OF BROWN ALGAE

At the Kunsthochschule Berlin Weissensee (KHB), the textile designer Juni Sun Ney-enhuys is also exploring the potential of algae. In her project "AL G. – Transformation of brown algae", she uses attractive textile designs to highlight the aesthetic variety of colours that the green raw material has. While E.S. Stevens described how bioplastics are produced from algae or alginate, vinegar and glycerine in his book "Green Plastics", no designer has previously successfully transformed this mixture into yarn. The result-ing textiles are unique fabrics that not only look beautiful, but also offer new potential alternatives for fast fashion.

MATERIALS MADE WITH ORGANIC WASTE

A clear trend towards closed material cycles in production processes has been emerging over the past few years among many small companies and designers. A major source of material is waste material from the food industry and agricultural waste from harvesting. Compared to conventional materials, agricultural waste has some key advantages: it is produced in large quantities, is freely available and can be recycled in a sustainable manner.

POTATO CORK

The potato tuber has several layers: the flesh that stores starch, the vascular ring and the outer skin. The skin, also known as cork cambium, protects the tuber against infections and excessive moisture loss, and is composed of lignin, cellulose, hemicellulose and protein, which together account for about 75 % of the dry matter of potato cork. The designers Rowan Minkley and Robert Nicoll from London use waste materials such as potato peel and starch from the manufacturers of crisps and potato chips to produce a pollutant-free particle board that they call "Chip[s] Board", a material that can be simply disposed of in conventional composting plants after use.

Furniture made from potato
peel as biomass
Source: Jarrell Goh

Surfboard made from agave
plant material
Source: Gary Linden Surfboards

POTATO CHAIR

Jarrell Goh from Singapore uses potato peel to create his design objects. After puréeing
the potato peel, white starch settles in the cloudy liquid and can simply be skimmed
off. In combination with dried and crushed potato peel, it is boiled into a doughy mass
to activate the binding effect of the starch. Pressing the mass into shape and renewed
drying results in a solid material product that can easily be composted after use.

AGAVE WASTE FROM TEQUILA PRODUCTION

In cooperation with the tequila producer José Cuervo, the US-American Gary Linden
has developed "100% Agave", a process and production model for surfboards made
entirely of waste material resulting from the distillation of tequila. The core of the
agave surfboard consists of wooden planks from the agave tree. To encase the wood,
Linden uses a textile layer won from agave pulp produced during the distillation of
tequila. This is extracted onto a sieve, formed around the wooden planks and dried
to a wood laminate. The syrup from the agave plant is then used to waterproof the
surfboard, thereby completely avoiding the use of toxic substances.

Lights, bottle coolers and
tiles by Tresta
Source: Katharina Hölz

Packaging made from tomato
fibres
Source: Jonas Emil Arndt

TOMATO FIBRES

The Dutch company Solidus Solutions produces cardboard trays and packaging boxes from tomato plant fibres. Once a year, large quantities of harvested tomato plants are cleared out of the greenhouses of Dutch tomato growers and up to now were composted. Fibres from paprika or cucumber plants are also suitable. The fibres are extracted and mixed with recycled waste paper to make paper in a process similar to that of conventional paper production.

TRESTA

The Rhineland-Palatinate region in Germany is known above all for its quality wines, which together account for more than 65 % of Germany's annual wine production. Where grapes are grown for wine production, waste materials such as stems, skins and seeds, known as pomace (or "Trester" in German), are also produced. Most of it ends up as unused biomass for composting or is used as fertiliser. In her master's thesis, the designer Katharina Hölz from Trier created objects using locally available biomass. In the spirit of the Cradle to Cradle principle, she has made lamps, wine bottle coolers and other interior furnishing objects out of dried, shredded pomace pressed into form using natural binding agents. The objects vary in colour depending on the grape variety and pressing. What they all share, however, is a pleasant smell of grape.

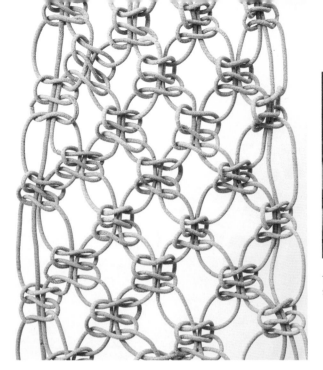

Textile made with orange peel
Source: Orange Fiber

Textile wood structures using
a lignin-based binder
Source: Esther Kaya Stögerer, Tilman
Holz, Nicole Dietz

ORANGE FIBER

Orange Fiber, a company based in Catania, Sicily, has developed a patented process to produce yarn and textile fabrics from orange peel. The two founders, Adriana Santanocito and Enrica Arena, based their production process on the observation that cellulose can be extracted from the peel of various citrus fruits. To convert the cellulose into yarn, they used further chemical reagents that made it possible to combine the yarn with other fibres such as cotton, silk or polyester.

REWOODABLE

In cooperation with the Fraunhofer Institute for Wood Research Wilhelm-Klauditz-Institut (WKI), Esther Kaya Stögerer, Tilman Holz and Nicole Dietz have developed wood composite materials that are free of harmful binders, do not emit toxic gases and can easily be returned to the material cycle. The project shows a variety of ways in which the lignin-based binders developed by the Fraunhofer Institute can be used with sawdust or wood shavings to make new products such as particle board, filaments for 3D printing or, when mixed with natural caoutchouc, flexible strands for textiles.

From nature to lampshade
and chairs
Source: Full Grown, Gavin Munro

BIOFABRICATION

While the term biofabrication is most commonly associated with the cultivation of organic tissue in Petri dishes, the term probably originates from the field of architecture in which hundreds of years ago so-called living bridges were made of roots, tendrils or lianas. Today, architects and designers are exploring ways of using living plants to create textile fabrics, design elements and even load-bearing components for furniture or architectural structures.

FULLGROWN

One of the current protagonists is the Englishman Gavin Munro, who grows fast-growing willow trees into unique furniture in a field in the British county of Derbyshire. No wood is sawn, and no wood glued; instead, the grown furniture is harvested straight from the field. The secret behind his fully-grown furniture is the training of the willow trees and branches using wires and cable ties to predefined shapes that guide the direction of growth. Depending on the size and desired stability of the end piece, the waiting time is between three and six years. When it comes to harvesting the furniture, the objects are freed from their supports, sawn off at the root and dried for about a year in the workshop before being finally sanded to achieve the distinctive natural wood look. More than 400 pieces of self-growing furniture are currently planted.

Arbo-architecture – grown junction without scaffolding
Source: Professor Ferdinand Ludwig, TU Munich

Arbo-architecture – stainless steel construction enclosed by wood
Source: Professor Ferdinand Ludwig, TU Munich

Interwoven – textile-like surfaces made by manipulating root growth
Source: Diana Scherer, Amsterdam; photo: Seed Soil Photography

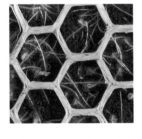

Interwoven – textiles created by controlling root growth
Source: Diana Scherer, Amsterdam; photo: Seed Soil Photography

ARBO-ARCHITECTURE

Ferdinand Ludwig from the TU Munich is growing architectural structures and was awarded the German Federal Prize for Ecodesign for his work in 2017. He combines biological and constructive principles to an architectural concept. Inspired by the visionary ideas of Arthur Wiechula – a German landscape architect who studied the growing structures of trees in nature some 100 years ago – Ferdinand Ludwig has been exploring the feasibility of arbo-architecture for several years. Wiechula's book "Growing Houses Emerging from Living Trees", published in 1926, described his experience and included sketches and details of how, for example, a branch can be bent with the help of a V-shaped incision so that it grows together again after being bent and fixed.

INTERWOVEN

The German artist Diana Scherer has sought ways to respond to depleting resources by exploiting biological growth processes for the waste-free production of textile structures. In her greenhouse in Amsterdam, she creates grass surfaces grown into predefined forms. Working together with Dutch scientists, she has struck on a way to precisely influence the pattern of root growth by varying certain parameters. Within a few weeks, an intricate root textile has grown that resembles an elaborately knotted macramé weaving.

BioBrick made using calcite-forming bacteria
Source: Haute Innovation

MycoTree – self-supporting lightweight construction made of mushroom material
Source: Professor Dirk Hebel, Philippe Block

BIO-BASED BUILDING MATERIALS

Stony coral
Source: Haute Innovation

The construction sector has particularly high energy and resource demands, due not least to the widespread use of concrete, a material that is almost universally employed around the world. The production of cement binders for concrete is extremely energy-intensive, and conventional cement works around the world emit more than one billion tonnes of carbon dioxide annually, which corresponds to 5% of global CO_2 emissions. Driven by the desire to reduce the enormous scale of emissions, scientists are striving to find suitable alternatives. Biochemists and biologists in particular are exploring several interesting approaches for bio-based binders.

MYCOTREE

Researchers at the ETH Zurich, KIT in Karlsruhe and the Singapore ETH Centre have used fungus-based building materials to create a three-dimensional branching structure made of load-bearing mycelium components for the 2017 Seoul Biennale. The "MycoTree" is a three-metre-high lightweight construction made of bamboo and mushroom mycelium that is even capable of supporting a 16 m² roof, likewise made of the same stiff grass material. According to the researchers, all the forces acting on the structure are optimally distributed not only by the choice of material but also by the design geometry.

In addition, the combination of fast-growing materials such as fungal mycelium and bamboo with dried plant residues as additives is a testament to the increasing importance accorded to avoiding waste in the construction industry, which over time looks set to render obsolete resource-intensive composites such as concrete.

Cement-free brick made of bacteria and urine
Source: UCT / Robyn Walker

Research team from Cape Town
Source: UCT / Robyn Walker

Instead, closed material cycles using such approaches may soon be within reach. A first potential application scenario, according to the researchers, could be predominantly temporary buildings that function as urban infill or ways of reactivating empty urban wasteland.

BIOBRICK

The American architect Ginger Krieg Dossier uses calcite-forming bacteria to produce a sustainable stone for the construction industry. The unusual development consists mostly of sand, a typical ingredient that in this case is not bound with water and cement, but with urine and a bacterium that is responsible for the growth of stony corals. In a biochemical process known as "microbial carbon precipitation", the bacteria separate the urea from the urine and form calcium carbonate. Solid bridges that can hold the sand together form within five days at room temperature, resulting in a stable, light grey composite. The large-scale production of BioBricks in North Carolina, USA, has since started successfully under the name "bioMason".

URINE BRICK

Scientists at the University of Cape Town are working on a similar approach to the production of cement-free biobricks. According to the South African researchers, the innovation in their development lies in the use of urine in its natural form. It is not synthetically produced and therefore requires little energy. In contrast to the BioBrick producers, who are already successfully producing their product, the scientists from Cape Town still have further development and optimisation phases ahead of them. Their main goal is to reduce the amount of urine required as much as possible. So far, the researchers need 25 to 30 l for one brick. Given an average quantity of 200 to 300 ml per toilet visit, this is a considerable amount. In addition, work is being conducted to improve the brick's stability, which, according to the current state of research, is about 40 % of that of a conventional lime-sand brick.

NEW MOBILITY CONCEPTS AND LIGHT-WEIGHT SOLUTIONS

The way we travel in urban environments is set to change profoundly as mobility concepts become smarter and above all more ecological. While mobility solutions in the 20th century were almost entirely dependent on the consumption of fossil fuels, the coming years will see a shift towards new approaches to mobility concepts. An increase in the use of electric vehicles is expected to reduce pollution in conurbations. However, the success of electric mobility will depend crucially on the extent to which developers succeed in significantly reducing the weight of components and in turn the use of resources. In addition, the use of materials based on renewable resources should significantly reduce the carbon footprint of vehicle and car body production.

It is no surprise that, alongside the automotive industry, the transport and aviation industries are major drivers of innovation in lightweight construction. In the case of aircraft, kerosene consumption represents a significant cost factor with respect to the overall life cycle. A central concern is therefore ways of reducing the weight of components, for example through the use of bionics, by exploiting the possibilities of additive production or using new materials. A 100 kg reduction in the dead weight of a passenger aircraft such as the A320 reduces kerosene consumption by around 10,000 l per year.

Consequently, lightweight solutions must always be considered in the context of their entire life cycle. This encompasses not just the product use phase but also its manufacture as well as the issue of disposal or recycling after use. Some materials, such as fibre-reinforced materials, offer advantages in weight reductions for the same or better strength and stiffness, while other materials, such as monomaterials, are currently gaining importance with regard to their recyclability.

Lightweight components made of high-tech woods
Source: Lignoa Leichtbau

In the context of new and forthcoming lightweight construction materials, two areas of development are of particular note. On the one hand, innovations are arising in material categories where new developments in lightweight construction were least expected, for example, the considerable number of new applications of wood for engineering semi-finished products or paper for use in composite materials. The other primary area is the development of lightweight construction solutions using natural, renewable or biotechnologically produced materials, or material innovations that draw inspiration from models of lightweight construction in nature.

A German company, for example, has succeeded for the first time in biotechnologically reproducing the extraordinary combination of material flexibility, tear resistance and light weight of spider silk and was able to apply these qualities to the upper material of a sports shoe. In Sweden, transparent hollow spheres made of wood cellulose have been produced for use as an admixture for composite materials, which can significantly reduce the resources used for packaging, components in biomedical engineering or in automotive engineering. And scientists from Saxony have succeeded in developing a production process for manufacturing tubes from wood for use in vehicle construction that have a weight comparable to that of carbon and a strength and stiffness better than aluminium.

PAPER COMPOSITE MATERIALS

The decline in print products in recent years has challenged the paper industry to find new areas of application for its technologies. A potential new market lies in the use of paper fibres and paper-based composites for lightweight construction.

PAPER COMPOSITES

In tests, scientists from the Fraunhofer Institute for Structural Durability and System Reliability (LBF) in Darmstadt were able to demonstrate that paper composites based on a thermoset matrix can exhibit mechanical strengths similar to those of natural fibres. To test the feasibility of substituting natural fibre composites with paper composites, the LBF scientists compared samples of laboratory paper and commercially available papers. The tensile tests were most promising: the results of the static load tests were significantly higher than those of tea paper, flax or viscose. If it proves possible to optimise further properties, such as flame resistance, insulation capacity and moisture absorption for the developed materials, it would open up a range of industrial applications in the sports sector, furniture construction and the automotive industry.

CARDBOARD HONEYCOMB CONSTRUCTIONS

Cardboard or paper honeycomb structures as core material for lightweight construction offer similar loading properties to comparable solutions made of aluminium, carbon or wood veneers. These chemically treated and dried paper honeycombs have a very low weight and offer excellent compressive strength. Through special coating and drying processes, cardboard honeycomb composites can be made water and fire resistant, making them suitable for use in vehicles, aircraft, shipping containers and mobile, modular houses.

COMPOSITE BUILDING MATERIAL OF
MINERAL-FILLED PAPER

LFS Board is a non-combustible lightweight composite board (fire protection class A) comprising a core of mineral-filled papers and fibre-reinforced facing layers. With a density of just 300 kg/m³, its weight is about quarter that of comparable fire protection boards on the market. Their low weight and high mechanical strength mean they have great potential for use in composite structures used in trade fair, ship and aircraft construction as well as for door panels, suspended ceilings or cladding panels.

Paper composite for sports applications
Source: Fraunhofer LBF

Paper composite material comprising a paper layer and thin-walled sheet metal
Source: PTS Group

Paper honeycomb panels with different cover layers and fillings
Source: BeeComp

Production of a Wikkelhouse
Source: Wikkelhouse Amsterdam

PAPER SHEET METAL

Paper sheet metal is a multifunctional composite material comprising thin-walled, high-strength sheet metal, a paper layer and an impregnated moulded fibre body based on cellulose fibres. The composite material has a low weight with good vibration damping behaviour and crash absorption qualities and exhibits good drapability and drainage capacity as well as being resistant to environmental influences. The use of resin in combination with paper as a fibrous material made it possible to reduce the weight of the overall composite significantly compared to pure sheet metal. By using water-repellent, flame-retardant or flame-resistant finishes and reducing heat conduction and viscoelastic behaviour, paper components can be given additional functions. Possible variants include functional printing with conductive strips or the application of RFID chips.

PAPER-WRAPPED ARCHITECTURE

The Wikkelhaus was developed by Dutch architects and designers to exploit the potential of cardboard as a lightweight material not normally associated with building for a modular architecture concept. Each 1.2-m-long module comprises a steel structural frame wrapped 24 times with recycled cardboard. From outside, a Wikkelhaus looks much like other conventional prefabricated houses as it is protected against the elements by a breathable membrane and wood cladding. Compared with other buildings, however, it requires just a third of the material and energy resources, with a service life of at least 100 years. A complete house consists of a maximum of eight modules and weighs just 6,000 kg.

Wikkelhouse
Source: Wikkelhouse Amsterdam

Cross-section of wall with
corrugated cardboard core
Source: Wikkelhouse Amsterdam

Residue-free biodegradable
plastic sports bottle
Source: Bayonix

BIODEGRADABLE BOTTLES

A vast amount of plastic waste floats around in the oceans of the world. The movements of the main ocean currents have created five large areas of waste accumulation, the largest of which is the so-called "Great Pacific Garbage Patch" off North America. In 2018, researchers revised their previous estimation of the quantity of marine debris in the oceans upwards. The garbage patch in the Pacific alone is said to amount to 80,000 t of plastic. In ice cores taken in 2015 near the North Pole, researchers from the Helmholtz Institute measured 12,000 microplastic particles per litre of sea ice.

In order to curb further pollution of the world's oceans, various countries have begun to ban plastic bags, disposable tableware, plastic straws and microplastics in cleaning products and toothpaste. In addition to optimising waste management logistics systems, materials producers are also working on lightweight biodegradable packaging for mass consumption.

BAYONIX BOTTLE
The Bayonix bottle, developed by a start-up from Bavaria, is the first plastic drink bottle that is completely biodegradable without polluting groundwater or nature. The material used for the bottle, cap, closure and all its constituents such as polymers, additives, catalysts and colour masterbatches are environmentally friendly and non-toxic for biological life cycles. The bottle can also be recycled because all its materials are suitable for upcycling and have no negative impact on conventional production processes. The Bayonix bottle is a monomaterial product and consists exclusively of a single polymer material.

GREEN FIBER BOTTLE

The Green Fiber Bottle is a paper-based alternative to PET bottles developed by a Danish producer. The bottle is made of 98% recycled paper and additional virgin organic fibres. A coating of casein, starch and PLA (polylactic acid) creates an oxygen barrier, while a nanocoating of silicone oxide or carbon gives the bottle its resistance to moisture. A special press was developed for the bottle's production that shapes the paper mass and extracts moisture from the material compound in 0.3 seconds. The Green Fiber Bottle is only half the weight of a comparable PET bottle.

Green Fiber Bottle – a paper bottle with a waterproof inner coating
Source: ecoXpac

CH₂OOSE Water – a paper alternative to PET bottles with a screw cap
Source: CH₂OOSE Water

CH₂OOSE WATER

The British developer James Longcroft has taken a similar approach. His CH₂OOSE Water bottle uses no plastics and the outer shell is made entirely of recycled paper that has been de-inked and cleansed. To create the moisture barrier, Longcroft has developed a liner made exclusively of natural materials that is suitable for both marine and soil environments. The metallic screw cap likewise decomposes without harming our ecosystem.

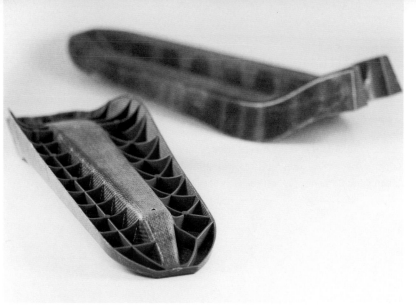

Bicycle luggage rack made of
a natural-fibre composite
Source: TU Dresden

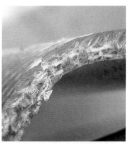

Organic sheet made of natural fibres
Source: TU Dresden

TEXTILE-BASED LIGHTWEIGHT CONSTRUCTION

The journey range of electric vehicles depends to a large degree on their weight. In recent years, heavy metallic structural elements are therefore being replaced by fibre-reinforced plastic parts. So-called organic plastic sheets are increasingly being used as panel-shaped, thermoformable semi-finished products.

ORGANIC PLASTIC SHEETS MADE OF NATURAL FIBRES

Conventional material composites typically consist of glass, carbon or aramid fibres in a petrochemical-based thermoplastic matrix. In view of the depletion of fossil resources, the TU Dresden investigated various alternative materials for organosheets and developed a biopolymer matrix to which a structure of natural fibres was added. The naturally good adhesion between natural fibres and biopolymers obviated the need for an additional adhesion promoter. The resulting composite materials have a low weight and do not splinter or form sharp edges in the event of a crash or damage. In addition, they are better at dampening vibrations, have a sound-absorbing effect and have a significantly more favourable energy balance.

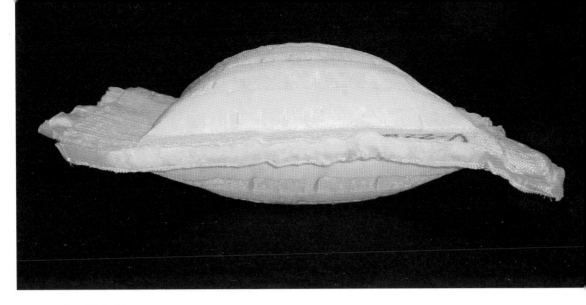

Spacer textiles with double-
curved fabric structures
Source: ITV Denkendorf

SPACER TEXTILES WITH DOUBLE-CURVED FABRIC STRUCTURES

Fibre-reinforced fabric structures are now not only sufficiently strong and stiff for use in industrial applications but are also increasingly flexible enough to be freely shaped into curvilinear geometries. Scientists at the Institute for Textile Technology and Process Engineering in Denkendorf, Germany, have developed new methods for producing very lightweight sandwich or hollow structures that enable not only the manufacture of regular plane-parallel spacer fabrics but also double-curved textile structures. The researchers drew inspiration from the skeleton of the sand dollar sea urchin and transferred the principle to curved spacer fabrics. This species of sea urchin possesses a curved outer shell with thin inner struts that make the shell very lightweight but also pressure resistant. In production, this was achieved by adapting the process of a double-rapier knitting machine to accommodate variable length spacer threads.

BIO-BASED, SELF-REINFORCING POLYMER COMPOSITES

To minimise recycling difficulties at the end of a product's useful lifetime, textile experts at RWTH Aachen University have developed bio-based, self-reinforcing composite materials made of a single polymer family. The resulting self-reinforcing polymer composites (SRPCs) exhibit characteristics that far exceed those of PLA (polylactic acid) panels with respect to brittleness and impact resistance. This can be attributed to the molecular structure of semi-crystalline areas retained in the material structure. The matrix is created, for example, by localised fusing of the reinforcing fibres. A major advantage over conventional composite fibre materials is that the SRPC comprises just one polymer family, which greatly simplifies recycling.

CNT-reinforced ceramic
Source: Fraunhofer IKTS

STABLE CARBON MODIFICATIONS

A large number of carbon-based materials with extraordinary qualities have found their way into industrial applications in recent years. Fullerenes, carbon nanotubes (CNTs) and graphene are stable modifications of elemental carbon that, in combination with other materials, can give conventional materials unusual properties.

CNT-REINFORCED CERAMICS

Due to their exceptional strength as reinforcing components, carbon nanotubes can significantly improve the mechanical properties of lightweight construction. Various applications have been developed in recent years, especially in the plastics sector. For ceramics and metals, however, their potential has until now only rarely been exploited due to the difficulty of binding carbon nanotubes to the matrix materials in the sintering process. Scientists at the Fraunhofer Institute for Ceramic Technologies and Systems (IKTS) have since succeeded in optimising the manufacturing process so that CNT matrix composites can be used for industrial lightweight construction. After catalytic activation, the CNTs grow on the matrix powder creating a strong bond with the surface of the powder.

GRAPHENE BATTERIES FOR ELECTRIC VEHICLES

Graphene consists of a single layer of hexagonally arranged carbon atoms. In addition to its extreme strength, it also exhibits high electrical conductivity. Scientists have devised a rechargeable battery as a capacitor made of two graphene layers that can potentially offer 50-100 times higher power density and 5-10 times more energy density than conventional rechargeable batteries. In addition, such batteries would be able to release a large amount of energy in a very short time. With these qualities, graphene batteries would give electric mobility an enormous boost, but the production of graphene material for batteries has until now been both costly and problematic due to its high reactivity and tendency to clump. In autumn 2017, however, Samsung announced a major breakthrough: using graphene-coated nanoscale spheres made of silicon dioxide, they were able to circumvent the problems involved in producing single graphene layers. In tests, lithium batteries made using graphene nanoballs as the anode material and cathode coating charged in just twelve minutes and exhibited a 28 % increase in energy capacity.

LIGHTWEIGHT GRAPHENE CONSTRUCTION

Until the breakthrough of graphene-based applications on a wider scale, experts expect graphene to be used in composite structures with other materials. Initial developments have already emerged in the sports sector. In mid-2016, the British bicycle manufacturer Dassi presented a carbon bicycle frame with a 1 % graphene content that weighs just 750 g. According to the manufacturer, graphene leads to a better carbon-resin bond giving the frame 70 % higher interlaminar shear strength and 50 % greater break resistance.

CARBYNE

Alongside carbon nanotubes and graphene, carbyne is another material under development that is expected to be stronger and harder than any other known material. Its basis is likewise carbon atoms, arranged not in a honeycomb pattern like graphene but in linear carbon chains. Due to its high reactivity, it has as yet been detected only by scientists at Rice University in the USA and at the Max Planck Institute in Hamburg. Initial research has revealed several characteristics of the new material, including that carbynes are expected to have twice the tear strength and toughness as graphene. Its exceptional electrical conductivity makes it predestined for use in nanoscale electronic components or solar cells.

Lignin-based carbon fibres
Source: Fraunhofer IAP

CARBON FIBRES FROM LIGNIN OR CARBON DIOXIDE

Carbon fibres have exceptionally good mechanical properties that make them particularly suitable for use as reinforcement in composite materials for lightweight construction. Although carbon fibres are highly stable and extremely lightweight, they are too cost-intensive to manufacture for many large-scale applications. At present, carbon fibres are obtained primarily from fossil-based polyacrylonitrile (PAN) or pitch. Alternative sources are currently being researched.

LIGNIN-BASED CARBON FIBRES

Bio-based production processes based on lignin offer a potentially more cost-effective alternative for the production of carbon fibres. Lignin is a hardening substance in the cell walls of wood cellulose with a carbon content of 55 to 65 % and is produced in large quantities as waste material in the paper industry, for example. Experts estimate that lignin-based carbon fibres would cost only half as much to manufacture as current methods. This would enable the application of carbon fibres to expand from its current niche of specialist applications in sports, aviation and boat building to mass markets for the automotive sector. At the Fraunhofer Institute for Applied Polymer Research (IAP), scientists are working on a lignin-based carbon fibre that has a tensile strength of 1.5 GPa and a tensile modulus of 150 GPa, which would therefore make it suitable for use in aviation.

116

Carbon fibres based on
carbon dioxide

Source: George Washington
University

CARBON FIBRES FROM CARBON DIOXIDE

Scientists at George Washington University in the USA are working on an alternative raw material source for the production of carbon fibres from the greenhouse gas carbon dioxide. The basis is a crucible filled with molten lithium carbonate. The researchers immerse a steel electrode and a nickel electrode in an electrolyte with selected additional metals. After the addition of lithium dioxide, carbon dioxide is supplied, and an electrical voltage is applied to the melt. The lithium dioxide reacts with the inflowing carbon dioxide to form lithium carbonate, which decomposes into lithium oxide, oxygen and carbon in the ensuing electrolysis. As a result, thin carbon fibres with a length of up to $200\,\mu m$ are deposited on the steel electrode.

At the AlgaeTec facility of the Technical University of Munich, a process is being developed to convert carbon dioxide into carbon fibres with the aid of algae. The algae first convert CO_2 into algae oil, from which the scientists can produce polyacrylonitrile fibres (PAN). These are then burnt into carbon-fibres in a carbon-neutral process utilising parabolic sun mirrors. The resulting fibres have the same mechanical and chemical properties as conventional carbon fibres available on the market.

Wood veneer tubes of
different diameters and wall
thicknesses
Photo: Haute Innovation

LIGHTWEIGHT TIMBER CONSTRUCTION

With 11.4 million ha of forest, Germany is one of the most densely wooded countries in the European Union. Wood is currently experiencing a renaissance in the building industry. Its specific material properties also make it interesting for technical applications. In recent years, numerous wood-based materials have been developed that can be used for mobile lightweight construction.

WOOD VENEER TUBES

Wood veneer tubes have an unusually high mechanical strength, strong enough even for use as a frame material for bicycles. They consist of several layers of real wood veneer that are cross-laminated and tightly compressed and are as such similar in structure to thin-layer plywood. Wall thicknesses of between 1 and 10 mm are possible depending on the number and thickness of the individual layers, and the material can be individually adapted to the requirements of a specific application. As with other laminar composite materials, the angle of fibre orientation can also be adjusted. The wood veneer tubes are available with inner diameters ranging from 20 to 100 mm in 5 mm steps and can be worked with virtually all common woodworking tools.

Willow seat shells
Source: BAU KUNST ERFINDEN,
Forschungsplattform der Universität
Kassel

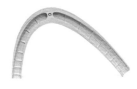

Lightweight components
made of high-tech woods
Source: Lignoa Leichtbau

WOODEN 3D TUBING

Under the name "Wooden 3D Tubing", the TU Dresden has developed a process for producing high-tech woods for the automotive industry that have a higher mechanical stability than aluminium and are as light as carbon. For the production of tubes and three-dimensionally curved wood components, thin veneer strips are placed on a mould and bent and bonded together. By exploiting the natural orientation of wood fibres in the longitudinal direction, components can be made that have particular tensile and breaking strength properties in the direction of the grain. In a second step, this component is cut into strips across the grain. These preformed pieces are placed in layers in a new form and once again bonded together. The resulting wooden components can withstand unusually high forces in both longitudinal and transverse directions. The moulded parts are then cut down the middle and hollowed out by milling the inward-facing surface to achieve the desired ratio of weight, stiffness and strength. A similar process is used for the manufacture of carbon structures for aviation.

ULTRALIGHT MOULDED WILLOW WOOD PARTS

Willow grows in almost all European natural habitats and has become known as a renewable high-tech material. SALIX 3D, developed at the University of Kassel in Germany, is a new lightweight construction method for the production of dimensionally stable and elastic shaped wood parts made of willow. Using machines specially developed for the process, willow strips or withies are arranged on flat surfaces to create fabrics, scrims or lattices precisely designed to resist the loads applied to them and then pressed into form under temperature and pressure. The resulting moulded elements are up to 40 % lighter than conventional moulded wood elements with the same load-bearing capacity. The material can be used in architecture, design and lightweight vehicle construction.

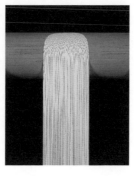

karuun rattan composite for
furniture construction
Source: out for space

karuun rattan composite with
translucent properties
Source: out for space

LIGHTWEIGHT RATTAN CONSTRUCTION

Rattan is a traditional and widely-used material for the manufacture of wickerwork products and seating furniture. It is harvested from the trunk of the fast growing Rotang palm, is very lightweight and can be bent easily through the application of heat and moisture. This is due to the high porosity and the large number of capillaries inside the shoots, which the plant uses to transport water over distances of up to 200 m. Under the name "karuun", designers from southern Germany have developed a process that improves the hardness, stiffness and resistance of the material by injecting fillers. When produced as a surface material, rattan has a translucent, light-permeable quality.

Bicycle with bamboo frame
Source: myBoo

LIGHTWEIGHT BAMBOO CONSTRUCTION

Thanks to its outstanding mechanical qualities, bamboo is the basis for a range of pioneering new materials. Known for its great strength, bamboo is also one of the fastest growing plants in the world, some species growing up to one metre per day. At the same time, it stores more CO_2 than any other plant. As bamboo is increasingly replacing metal in many constructions, this natural product has earned the name Green Steel. Its fibres are flexible and very resistant to tensile stress. It has been used for centuries in Asia as a sustainable and cost-effective building material and is now also being rediscovered in Europe.

Bamboo transport pallet
made of panels with a core
layer of bamboo ring sections
Source: Conbou

Bamboo sandwich panels
Source: Fabian Schütz, Denkfabrik Bambus

A prosthetic running blade made as a bamboo sandwich construction
Source: Fabian Schütz, Denkfabrik Bambus

BAMBOO SANDWICH CONSTRUCTIONS

Due to its organic growth and irregular formation, bamboo has been used only rarely in industrial applications. Bamboo-based materials must therefore be developed to meet regulatory standard requirements. In combination with natural core materials such as cork, balsa, wood fibres or PLA honeycombs, bamboo sandwich constructions represent a lightweight alternative for many typical lightweight applications.

BOOGLUE

BooGlue is a new patented industrial adhesive based on natural raw materials that has the potential to replace conventional isocyanates (MDI, TDI, HDI), urea-formalde-hyde (UF) and polyurethane adhesives (PU, PUR). The concept originates from Costa Rica and was developed in particular for the manufacture of substitute wood materials using bamboo fibres. BooGlue is a thermosetting two-component adhesive that is non-toxic during manufacture as well as after use. According to the manufacturer, its strength, durability and user-friendliness compare favourably with other conventional adhesives.

JOBAM hexagonal bamboo tubes
Source: Robert Klanten

Bamboo hybrid fabric
Source: Fabian Schütz, Denkfabrik Bambus

Bamboo chipboard
Source: Möbelfabrik Bard

HEXAGONAL BAMBOO TUBE

As naturally grown bamboo canes vary in size, diameter and thickness, they have been hard to harness for industrial uses. With the help of a patented production process, the diameter as well as the thickness and length of bamboo elements can now be adjusted with industrial precision. This method makes it possible, for example, to produce hexagonal bamboo tubes with comparable mechanical qualities to aluminium tubes. As such, they have the potential to be a sustainable alternative to many applications in architecture, construction, structural engineering or vehicle construction where metal constructions are still state of the art.

BAMBOO CHIPBOARD

After several years of development, the furniture producer Bard from Switzerland has presented a bamboo reinforced chipboard that is three times stronger than comparable board materials. Made using whole bamboo canes, longitudinally split cane segments or splinters, bamboo chipboard has the potential to significantly reduce the quantity of material used in furniture and shipbuilding. The structure of the board material can be adapted to the respective application, and several layers of bamboo can be bonded into multiple plies.

BAMBOO HYBRID FABRIC

Bamboo fibres have unique damping properties and are both stiff and flexible. In hybrid fabrics, biaxial thin layers of bamboo fibres are paired with cork, balsa or honeycomb cores to form torsionally and flexurally stiff sandwich materials. Fabrics made of bamboo and carbon fibres have a lower weight and very high strength and can be used as an organic sheet material for car bodies, as prepregs for wind turbine blades or in the outer bodywork of train carriages.

Concrete with bamboo reinforcement
Source: KIT, Professor Dirk Hebel,
photo: Carlina Teteris

BAMBOO-REINFORCED CONCRETE

At the Future Cities Laboratory (FCL) in Singapore and the Karlsruhe Institute of Technology (KIT), researchers are working to unlock the potential of bamboo through
the development of new types of bamboo composites for the construction industry
and transport and mobility applications. The material's tensile strength inspired Dirk
Hebel's team to examine the use of fibres and strips of natural bamboo as (sustainable) reinforcement variants for structural concrete.

Hollow glass spheres
Source: 3M

HOLLOW SPHERES

The compact spherical geometry of hollow spheres makes them particularly pressure-resistant and rigid. In addition, hollow spheres are 40 to 70% lighter than solid spherical masses and can contribute significantly to reducing a material's weight. In recent years, metallic and ceramic hollow spheres have been used in the production of heat exchangers, catalytic converters or as crash absorbers and silencers, and current research is exploring solutions for lightweight construction.

HOLLOW GLASS SPHERES

With a density of just 0.46 g/cm³, hollow glass spheres from 3M are predestined for applications in the context of lightweight construction. Depending on filling degree and formulation, they can reduce the weight of plastic systems by up to 30%. Further advantages of this new type of filling material in composite materials are its good thermal insulation and quick cooling properties. In a joint study with 3M, the vehicle engineering company EDAG identified applications in vehicle interiors, exteriors and engine compartments in which hollow glass spheres offer specific advantages. In injection moulding tests, for example, using hollow glass spheres as a filler had a positive effect on the manufacturing process, cycle time and thus on cost-effectiveness compared with other filler compounds.

Hollow cellulose spheres with
porous shells
Source: Cellutech

HOLLOW CELLULOSE SPHERES

Cellutech from Sweden has developed a variety of hollow spheres made of pure cellulose. Depending on the manufacturing method, the spheres range in size from a few hundred micrometres to a few millimetres and exhibit different properties. The very low density of the spheres can significantly contribute to reducing the weight of material compounds. Possible applications include packaging, medical technology, life science and cosmetics. Cellulose spheres are available with water-impervious solid shells that make them buoyant or with water-permeable porous outer walls.

Hybrid panel with cellulose
foam core
Source: Fraunhofer IFAM

BIO-BASED FOAMS

A multitude of lightweight but simultaneously high-strength materials in nature exploit the mechanical qualities of foams and sponges. In the context of sustainability and lightweight construction, one can see a clear trend towards bio-based foams made from renewable raw materials.

HYBRID PANEL WITH CELLULOSE FOAM CORE

This sandwich panel is made of wood particles and foamed cellulose bioplastic. As a hybrid panel, it consists of a lightweight foam core sandwiched between two high-density facing layers. Using bioplastics for the foam core in place of the usual polystyrene foam results in an environmentally friendly, resource-saving and lightweight material. The sandwich panel represents a new approach for using wood and opens up new areas of application for by-products of the wood industry.

Cellufoam made of nano-
cellulose
Source: Cellutech

Bicycle helmet with Cellufoam
Source: Cellutech

NANOCELLULOSE FOAM

Under the name "Cellufoam", Swedish scientists have developed a foam made of nanocellulose and used it as cushioning in a crash helmet. Made of cellulose, the foam is biodegradable and has excellent shock-absorption properties making it suitable for many applications where lightweight construction and damage protection are important, such as in packaging material and safety applications. The idea for the foam came from a research group at the Wallenberg Wood Science Center (WWSC) and was developed further by Cellutech.

FOAM STRUCTURES FROM SEA SPONGES

Over the course of millions of years, structures of natural plants and living creatures have developed that offer great potential for research and industry in their ongoing attempts to develop resource-saving lightweight constructions. For example, the structure of mussel shells, corals and sea sponges offers great potential for adapting to industrial applications, as they are not only extremely lightweight, but also very resilient and remarkably mobile. Glass sponges found at depths of 5,000 m are even capable of conducting light and consist of needle-shaped skeleton elements that form only under very specific environmental conditions. Through biomineralisation, scientists are currently trying to emulate the natural growth processes in the sea with a view to applying them to the fields of automotive engineering, architecture and medicine.

Running shoe with upper
surface made of biotechnologically produced spider silk
Source: ADIDAS

SILK MATERIALS

The silk thread produced by spiders is a textbook example of the principle of bionics. More resilient than steel and as elastic as rubber, it is nature's high-tech material. After AMSilk and Thomas Scheible succeeded in biotechnologically engineering spider silk proteins from genetically modified bacteria in a fermentation process, Adidas presented its first example of "Biofabric" in late 2016 in the form of a running shoe with an upper surface made of spider silk. It is one of the first consumer goods to perfectly represent a closed biological cycle: while the textile material remains stable under the influence of water, it can be dissolved in a concentrate of the digestive enzyme proteinase and will decompose naturally within 36 hours. In addition, the spider silk makes the shoe 15 % lighter.

In the context of biological value creation in industry, silk materials are gaining increasing importance and have become the subject of research across the globe. Now that scientists are able to produce silk proteins of high quality in high quantities, a range of new applications is emerging, for example in the production of sponges, transparent foils and nanofibres for use in lightweight construction.

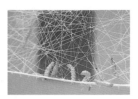

Silk pavilion made of silk thread
Source: MIT Media Lab

ARCHITECTURE WITH SILKWORMS

Silkworm fibres are the traditional source of the silk we know from textiles. The aim of the "Silk Pavilion" research project at MIT Media Lab in the USA was to apply this to architecture. The concept of biologically inspired fabrication was based on the way silkworms create a cocoon from a single strand of silk. For the pavilion of the research project, a steel frame structure consisting of 26 polygonal panels was first erected and wrapped by a robot with an approximately one-kilometre-long silk thread. 6,500 silkworms were then placed on the woven structure and the caterpillars were allowed to follow their natural instincts. The caterpillars began to close the gaps with silk. In the process, the researchers observed a connection between the activity of the silkworms, the position of the sun and the size of the gaps. The researchers recorded the movement preferences of the silkworms in a sun-path diagram along with the differences in the density of the silk fibres.

SILK FROM PHOLCID SPIDERS

A group of researchers from Trento, Italy, has succeeded in producing spider silk from pholcid spiders with a tensile strength three times higher than usual. The properties of this new form of spider silk exceed even those of aramid fibres and could have enormous potential for lightweight construction and aviation. The spiders were sprayed with water enriched with carbon nanotubes and graphene and the researchers found that the resulting silk incorporated the nanoparticles arranged within the silk thread.

Silk from honeybees
Source: CSIRO; photo: David McClenaghan

SILK FROM HONEYBEES

In addition to spiders and silkworms, other insects also produce this high-quality fibre, which serves an important protective function during pupation. Honeybee larvae, for example, produce the silk thread in their labial glands. Australian scientists led by Dr Tara Sutherland at the Commonwealth Scientific Industrial Research Organisation (CSIRO) have succeeded in identifying the genes of silk proteins, reproducing them biotechnologically and deriving them for high-quality lightweight fibres. Further studies focus on investigating the essential design elements of silk genes in bumblebees and ants.

GREEN LACEWING SILK

To protect them from predators, green lacewing flies deposit their eggs on the underside of leaves on the ends of highly-stable silk threads. The fibres, known as egg stalks, are only 15 µm thick and are produced by the insects as a protein secretion deposited on the leaves. The egg is laid in the droplet and then pulled out perpendicularly from the leaf. The resulting silk thread then hardens in the air. The Fraunhofer Institute for Applied Polymer Research (IAP) is currently working on a process to biotechnologically reproduce lacewing silk proteins. The experiments are based on preliminary molecular-biological work conducted in recent years by Thomas Scheibel at the Department of Biomaterials at the University of Bayreuth. The result is a special gene sequence which enables E. coli bacteria to reproduce the silk protein in enzymes. As a highly rigid fibre, the material should in future be used in lightweight composites for applications in the mobility sector.

Silk of the lacewing fly
Source: Fraunhofer IAP

BIONIC STRUCTURES FROM THE SEA

Limpet
Photo: Stefan Thiesen

Researchers have increasingly been turning to the oceans as a source of analogies with potential for application to lightweight construction. For some years, scientists have been working on deciphering the secrets of natural models with a view to finding ways to increase resource efficiency.

THE HIGH-PERFORMANCE TEETH OF LIMPETS

Until recently, spider silk was thought to be the strongest natural material ever tested. But in 2015, British researchers from the University of Portsmouth discovered a new record holder in the form of the limpet and declared that limpet teeth are now the strongest known biological material. With a tensile strength of up to 4,900 MPa, limpet teeth can withstand ten times the forces that human teeth can and are comparable in strength to Kevlar fibres. The phenomenon can be attributed to the structure of the teeth, which consists of microscopic nanofibres embedded in a protein matrix. The transfer of this principle to industrial materials would make numerous lightweight solutions possible.

Mantis shrimp
Photo: University of California

MANTIS SHRIMPS AS A MODEL FOR LIGHTWEIGHT COMPOSITES

In the field of bionics, the mantis shrimp has long been regarded as a creature with special potential for aviation. This species of crustacean, known as smashers, kill their prey with the aid of club-like limbs that strike with an impact comparable to that of a bullet from a pistol. Their enormous acceleration force is a product of the specific structure of its exoskeleton that allows the clawed arms to propel forward rapidly, smashing the shells of their marine prey. Researchers at the University of California found that the highly compact herringbone structure has a multi-layered structure with a sinusoidal arrangement of chitin fibres in some parts that are mineralised with highly textured calcium phosphate. The ability to replicate the logic of this structure would offer great potential for high-strength composite structures for aerospace and military applications.

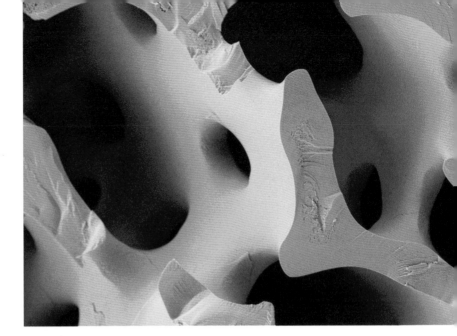

Structure of a sea urchin
spine
Source: University of Constance

Bending experiment
conducted on elastic cement
Source: University of Constance

HIGH-STRENGTH BUILDING MATERIALS
INSPIRED BY SEA URCHIN SPINES

Researchers at the University of Constance have developed a cement based on the
structure of a sea urchin spine. Consisting principally of lime, a fragile and brittle
material, the high stability of the spine is a product of the microscopic structure in
which ordered crystalline layers of lime are embedded in softer, amorphous layers of
calcium carbonate. When subject to a load, the spine transfers compressive energy
from the brittle areas to the softer layers. Where conventional concrete achieves a
breaking strength of between 2 and 5 MPa, the nanostructured cement of a sea
urchin's spine has a breaking strength of 200 MPa. Similar principles can also be found
in mussel shells and bones.

5

DIGITALISATION AND INTERNET CULTURE

Moulded part with integral sensor
Source: Fraunhofer IWU

The effects of digitalisation have gained increasing economic importance in recent years. Initially, those industry sectors whose products were themselves part of the digital value chain (e. g. digital data media or playback devices) or those that could be easily digitised (e. g. music) were most affected by the disruptive changes to business models, but now other industries with conventional production and distribution systems are also feeling the effects of digital transformation. Traditional over-the-counter trade has been particularly affected and, despite additional digital sales instruments, is being called into question in its present form. Customers are increasingly making use of online shopping opportunities, in turn accelerating the digitalisation of trade and logistics.

Shape memory material as an information media
Source: Fraunhofer IAP

It is foreseeable that in future the production of goods will be triggered only when an order is placed. Thin film sensors and embedded microchips in material surfaces make it possible to connect products, machines and logistics systems to the web. In the Internet of Things, we are beginning to see self-organised intelligent production processes in which products, materials, logistics networks and disposal systems communicate with each other.

In this context, applications for digitally-augmented materials and surfaces with electrically conductive properties or integral electronic systems are starting to emerge, and material producers have begun equipping materials with these new surface properties. Whether for plastics, paper, textiles or human skin, the combination of different substances has made it possible to incorporate electrical circuits in unusual situations.

Developers and designers are coming up with ever more ways of using such special digital materials to digitally control our private environments. "Smart home" technology provides digital options to control heating or lighting, kitchen appliances or sun-shading devices. Materials such as touch-sensitive concrete or wooden surfaces that emit bluish-green light in the dark are further technically-advanced examples of digital materials in which data streams and electrical impulses have been incorporated.

An electronic circuit as tattoo
Source: Jimmy Day, MIT, USA

For some time now, scientists and designers have been working intensively towards turning the dream of flexible and extensible electronic products into reality by the simple and affordable means of printing circuits onto a variety of different materials. The term wearables has emerged over the last few years to describe technology for the digitalisation of clothing and fashion as well as electronic systems worn on the body. In future, the term will also encompass the use of personal robotics. Scientists have already successfully demonstrated the integration of artificial muscles into textile fabrics. The goal of developing flexible exoskeletons from textile materials will soon be within reach as further advances in material technology are made.

TouchCrete touch-sensitive
concrete surface
Source: BAU KUNST ERFINDEN –
Forschungsplattform der Universität
Kassel

MATERIALS FOR THE SMART HOME

In recent years, a whole series of systems have come onto the new Smart Home market aimed at increasing quality of life, security and energy efficiency by introducing digital solutions to the private realm. Lighting, electrical appliances, heating, blinds and alarm systems are ideally connected to the home's network so that they can be controlled via the internet or communicate with the homeowner. In addition to the IT system as a programmatic representation of the network, materials and coatings have been developed for specific tasks that incorporate sensor technology and data and light transmission within composite materials.

TOUCHCRETE

The University of Kassel has developed a technology for touch-sensitive concrete surfaces under the name "TouchCrete" that enables the incorporation of circuits in concrete so that wall surfaces can act as a touch-sensitive panel. Individually combinable actuator-sensor components along with a corresponding control unit are integrated into a textile-reinforced concrete surface that connects to the W-LAN network and is functionally programmable. Touching or swiping the concrete surface can be used to switch lighting on and off or to control the volume of the hi-fi system.

Glass surfaces with SensGlass
coating
Source: Future-Shape

SENSGLASS

SensGlass coating makes glass surfaces usable as sensors. The glass surface consists of laminated safety glass with a conductive and highly transparent coating. The radio module contains a capacitive proximity sensor connected to the conductive glass surface. If a body or object approaches the glass surface, a sensor signal is activated which can be transmitted by radio. This can be used to trigger an alarm system, open a door or switch on the lights.

LIGHT-EMITTING FIBRE-OPTIC CONCRETE

By embedding fibre-optic cables in concrete and supplying them via a corresponding control system, the Berlin-based start-up SIUT has created a concrete composite that can transmit points of light in all directions. The optical fibres can be individually controlled and emit points of light on any visible surface of the concrete material. When used as a means of controlling commercially available LEDs, fibre-optic concrete can be employed as a digital wayfinding and guidance system.

zlinn wireless office light
powered by wireless WiTech
technology
Design: Dietmar Lorenz

INDUCTIVE SYSTEMS

With the advent of smart solutions in office environments and private households, wireless energy transmission systems are becoming more and more important. The production of an electric field after a change in the magnetic flux density is termed electromagnetic induction.

CORIAN CHARGING SURFACE

To achieve wireless charging for smartphones or tablets on office, kitchen and bathroom surfaces made of the mineral material Corian, the chemical company DuPont has developed a solution that is completely invisible beneath the monolithic surface of the material. The energy transmitter is mounted in a recess on the reverse of the Corian worktop. With the help of an adapter ring, different mobile devices can then be charged within a specific area of the surface.

A levitating FLYTE light
Source: FLYTE

Mobile device with adapter
ring for charging with energy
Source: DuPont

WITECH WIRELESS

The Fraunhofer Institute for Electronic Nano Systems (ENAS) has developed a technology for energy transmission by electromagnetic induction that covers an entire table surface and can supply various devices with energy. Unlike other systems, the mobile device to be charged – such as a desk lamp or laptop – can be placed anywhere on the table. The table surface is equipped with a transmitter unit comprising a matrix of different coils, and energy transmission occurs with the help of an energy receiver placed on the surface.

FLYTE

The shatterproof LED light devised by a Swedish start-up in Stockholm employs the repulsive forces between magnetic fields to cause the light to levitate in the air and rotate slowly. The light can be switched on and off by simply touching the wooden surface. The light itself has no battery of its own. Once the wooden base is connected to the power supply, energy is transferred by induction through the air to the light source. The manufacturer says the light has a service life of around 50,000 hours.

Magnetisable asphalt road surface
Photo: Haute Innovation

MAGNETISABLE ROAD SURFACES

The days of the combustion engine are numbered and new visions for the future of mobility are gradually emerging. In inner-city situations and for supply logistics within conurbations, electric mobility looks set to become the dominant approach in the coming years. The biggest obstacle at present is the lack of infrastructure for recharging vehicles. Systems for integrating wireless energy transmission into the road surface represent a possible solution.

MAGNETISABLE CEMENT CONCRETES

The company Magment has developed material formulations for magnetisable cement-based concretes that can act as inductive energy transmitters. The material's magnetic qualities are achieved by adding ferrite particles from recycled material and electronic scrap to the cement matrix. Initial permeabilities of up to 60 can be achieved, enabling a very broad spectrum of electromagnetic applications. Cement is used as a binder wherever high mechanical resilience and high resistance to environmental influences are required.

MAGNETISABLE ASPHALT CONCRETES

While cement is commonly used as a binder where very high robustness is required, asphalt is chosen for cost reasons in cold climates or to reduce tyre noise. Magnetisable asphalt concretes are based on a special bitumen matrix containing magnetisable particles with which initial permeabilities of up to 40 can be achieved. Magnetisable concretes can be used for wireless energy transmission on asphalt roads as well as driveways and parking spaces. Efficiency levels of over 90 % have already been achieved with outputs of up to 500 kW.

Luminous surfaces made up
of a large number of light
points
Photo: Haute Innovation

MICROLEDS

MicroLEDs are tipped to be the energy-efficient successor to OLED organic light-emitting diodes with a significantly lower energy consumption. Rather than using a single luminous layer, the display technology employs a large number of microscopically small LEDs in the primary colours red, green and blue to represent the individual pixel elements. The principle is comparable to that of old CRT television sets, where the actual colour information of a pixel is composed of three subpixels.

Compared to conventional LCD displays, MicroLED screens offer significantly increased luminance, higher contrast ratios and faster switching times. The LEDs are manufactured from conventional gallium nitride, which can produce 30 times higher brightness levels. Because they require neither colour filters nor additional backlighting, they are also flatter and lighter, and have significantly increased efficiency in light and image generation. In addition, MicroLED displays are more robust and should be more durable.

Since the individual LEDs have to be microscopically small to fit millions of times on the carrier materials of the display, only limited technological breakthroughs have been made. For several years now, some of the large tech companies have been investing extensive personnel resources in research into economical manufacturing methods, as MicroLED technology promises to extend battery life and presents a way of making flexible displays for folding phones.

Electroluminescent facade
coating
Source: Inoviscoat

ELECTROLUMINESCENT LIGHT COATINGS

Light-emitting materials and substances have always held a special fascination for designers and architects. A special atmosphere can be created by actively illuminating the surfaces of facades. Similarly, in conjunction with textiles or wood, luminous furniture, curtains or illuminated wallpaper can also be created.

Multiple coating systems exist for equipping different substrates with luminous qualities. A coated flexible plastic film usually serves as the actual light source in which an electric current causes the entire film surface to glow evenly. Other substrates such as textiles, paper or even metal films can also be provided with luminous layers. The coating is applied on an industrial scale using roll-to-roll processing. All the necessary functional layers are individually chemically formulated and dispersed in water. They are then brought in contact as a package with the substrate.

In physical terms, the system is a plate capacitor. Current flows between the two electrodes and generates an electric field so that the pigments in the luminous layer are excited. The light radiates through the carrier substrate. Different colours are possible, and the light can be dimmed. The material, which is only 0.175 mm thick, can be cut to almost any shape and applied to surfaces.

Due to their great flexibility, electroluminescent coatings can also be used to equip sportswear, backpacks and tents. In other technology sectors, further solutions are conceivable in the fields of optics, safety engineering, pharmaceuticals and energy systems.

EAS product security tag
Source: ThinFilm

PRINTED ELECTRONICS

In the Internet of Things products, systems and goods communicate with each other. Logistical processes, orders and deliveries will be partially automated and can be controlled within the digital system. In this context, printed electronic solutions will play an increasingly important role as a straightforward means of providing surfaces with electronic functions and facilitating data transmission. To this end, conductive print media and smart labels are currently being developed that can fulfil various different functions.

ELECTRONIC PRODUCT SECURITY

ThinFilm from Oslo has launched a smart label for electronic product security in order to improve traditional electronic article surveillance (EAS) technology. The result is a new category of anti-shoplifting labels that are easy to incorporate into merchandise and are compatible with the world's 8.2 MHz radio frequency EAS infrastructure.

NFC BARCODE

ThinFilm has also developed a near field communication (NFC) barcode to facilitate communication between smartphones and everyday objects, including printed electronics. This principle opens up numerous possible applications in the interaction between customers and companies, helping to optimise logistical processes and improve service while also strengthening customer loyalty.

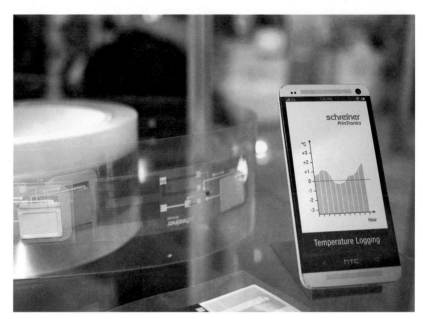

RFID packaging label for
sensitive foods
Source: Schreiner Prin-Tronics

RFID SENSORS IN THE COLD CHAIN OF SENSITIVE FOODS

In 2017, the Competence Center Schreiner PrinTronics presented the first printed RFID sensor platform in which printed packaging labels were equipped with electronic functions including a temperature sensor, an initial opening sensor and an NFC chip. The aim is to monitor and ensure the interruption-free continuity of supply chains and the cold chains of time- and temperature-sensitive products, such as foodstuffs or medicines. The printed NFC antenna makes the contactless reading of transport data possible using a suitably equipped smartphone.

PRINTED BATTERIES

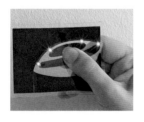

Printed battery for an LED as
a display element
Source: Fraunhofer ENAS

The Fraunhofer Institute for Electronic Nano Systems (ENAS) has developed a solution for a printed battery based on a zinc-manganese dioxide system that can be applied to a film substrate and is very flexible with respect to geometric shape, voltage, capacity and weight. With a thickness of less than one millimetre and an output of 2 mAh/cm², the layout can be adapted to the respective application. As such, it is particularly well-suited for thin and flexible products. Serial arrays of several batteries can be printed in a single operation to achieve voltages in the range of 1.5 to 6 V. Application areas include intelligent chips, sensor cards and medical plasters for monitoring body functions.

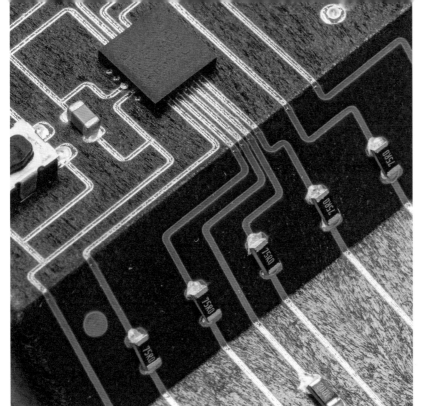

3D circuit board with printed circuit paths
Source: Neotech AMT GmbH

3D-printed cube with integrated circuits
Source: Neotech AMT GmbH

PRINTED SENSORS AND ANTENNAS

Using a patented technology for coating surfaces with conductive or insulating pastes and liquids, Neotech GmbH from Nuremberg has specialised in the development of production methods for printed electronic applications. With the help of additive production equipment and 3D printers, electronic components and systems can be applied to flat surfaces as well as complex three-dimensional shapes. Application areas for the technology include printed antennas for mobile radio applications, integrated sensors and materials for protecting and connecting sensitive electronics, as well as injection-moulded interconnect devices (3D-MID).

CONDUCTIVE PAPERS AND PRINTED PAPER ELECTRONICS

The manufacture of flexible electronic products is still very cost-intensive. Scientists are pursuing various alternative avenues that range from enhancing cost-effective materials for use as electronics to developing elastic and flexible circuits. A further vision for the future is the ability to print electronic circuits onto different substrates.

CONDUCTIVE INKS AND PASTES

In recent years, conductive polymers and inks have been developed for printed electronics that can be easily applied to large areas or printed on paper, plastic foil, textiles or glass surfaces. This would make the production of electronic components such as sensors, displays, RFID chips and smart labels much more cost-effective. Conductive metallic inks capable of transporting sufficient energy to supply LEDs with power are even available for fountain pens. The ink contains minute silver-plated copper lamella that arrange themselves in layers as they dry.

CIRQUIDS – LOW-TECH LED PAPER DISPLAY

Under the name "Cirquids", the designer Dorothee Clasen has developed a process for the production of low-tech displays on paper that does without the use of special chemicals for etching. Instead, wax, salt and water are used. With these simple elements, the designer has found a simple way of making paper conductive. Negative forms of the conductive tracks are defined in the paper, which only become conductive on contact with salt water. The circuit of the printed circuit board (PCB) is only closed when the paper is moistened, and its conductivity decreases accordingly over time. Two layers of paper circuits are printed on top of each other and parts that should have no contact are isolated with wax. To protect the paper from damage, it is also laminated. LED pins can then be pricked directly into the paper.

Low-tech LED display made of paper
Source: Dorothee Clasen

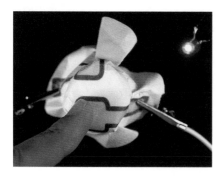

Touch-sensitive paper
Source: Dorothee Clasen

Kohpa carbon fibre paper
Source: RESO Oberflächentechnik

"Le pli" lamp made of folded
Kohpa carbon fibre paper
Source: RESO Oberflächentechnik;
design: Sascha dos Santos, Tilmann
Studinsky

Kohpa carbon fibre paper
Source: RESO Oberflächentechnik

KOHPA CARBON FIBRE PAPER

In addition to coating a substrate with a conductive paste or ink, papers can also be made electrically conductive by using carbon fibres in the manufacture of non-wovens. To this end, the so-called wet-laid process was optimised to facilitate an even distribution of carbon and cellulose fibres within the paper. The carbon fibres are recycled from resin-bonded carbon fibre reinforced plastic (CFRP) structures by thermo-chemical splitting (pyrolysis) and the paper fibres come from recycled waste. Kohpa carbon fibre paper is electrically conductive and can also be used as a heated surface, as temperatures in excess of 100 °C can be produced when a low-current voltage is applied. Carbon fibre paper can be laminated to shield other materials from electromagnetic radiation. It can be processed like a textile fabric.

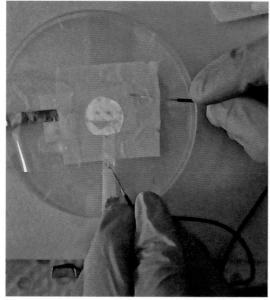

Luminous effect of the yellow
ionic coating
Source: South China University of
Technology

IONIC GEL COATING

In 2017, researchers at South China University of Technology presented a first look at
an inexpensively producible conductive paper that uses an ionic gel coating. At a price
of just over one euro per square metre, this flexible electronic material would make
it possible to mass-produce items such as roll-up screens or illuminated wallpapers.
The conductivity of the paper is a product of freely moving, charged ions that can
circulate in the ionic gel. When a voltage is applied, the paper glows in a shimmering
blue tone. So far, the ionic gel-coated paper has withstood more than 5,000 bending cycles. More research is needed, however, to extend the current shelf life of two
months.

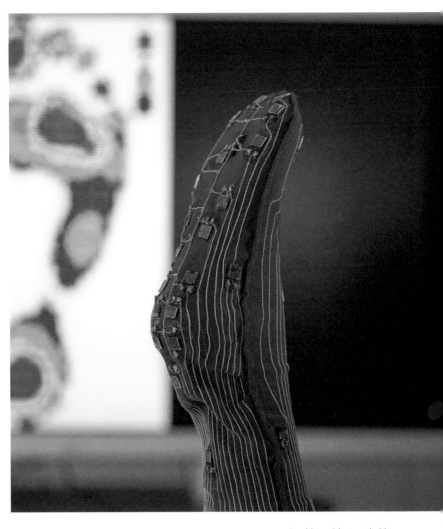

Stocking with stretchable dielectric sensor as wound protection for people with diabetes
Source: Fraunhofer ISC

ELASTIC CIRCUITS
FOR WEARABLES

In recent years, the term wearables has emerged to describe electronic technology systems worn on the body or integrated into clothing. An important aspect for the comfort of wearables and the development of TechFashion, is the development of electronic components that are flexible and elastic.

EXPANDABLE ELECTRONICS WITH LIQUID METAL

In 2016 at the École Polytechnique Fédérale de Lausanne (EPFL), researchers unveiled conductive tracks that can stretch to four times their length and bend in all directions. The tracks are made of an elastic polymer in which an alloy of gold and gallium is embedded. Gallium was chosen for its very low melting point of about 30 °C. Due to the phenomenon of undercooling, the alloy component remains liquid even at lower temperatures. The gold prevents the gallium from forming droplets when it comes into contact with the plastic so that the continuity of the conductive track is not interrupted. The scientists hope that the technology will enable them to integrate circuits into smart clothing or apply them directly to the skin. The conductive tracks can be as thin as a few hundred nanometres.

ELASTIC SENSORS

An interesting development of an elastic sensor comes from Danfoss in the Netherlands. The principle employs a dielectric elastomer consisting of a silicone film and a silver coating. Stretching the film causes its charge capacity to change and this can be used to detect physical changes such as pressure or stretching. Research into similar systems is also being conducted at the Fraunhofer Institute for Silicate Research (ISC) in Würzburg.

HYBRID 3D PRINTING FOR ELASTIC CIRCUITS

Scientists at Harvard University's Wyss Institute have developed a 3D printing process that can be used to print elastic circuits on textile fabrics. The printing material consists of a thermoplastic polyurethane with embedded silver particles. As part of the additive production process, the electronic circuits are applied using a vacuum print head after the polyurethane conductor tracks have been applied. To demonstrate the functionality, elastic sensors have been successfully integrated into shoes and the sleeves of outerwear.

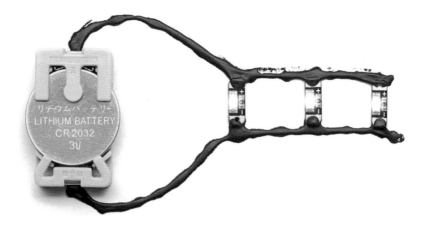

Electrically conductive ink
dries at room temperature
and is non-toxic
Source: Bare Conductive

PRINTED ELECTRONICS ON HUMAN SKIN

The possibilities for implementing electrical circuits and using electrical components are wide-ranging and can also be applied to human skin. A conductive, paste-like mass has, for example, been developed that makes it possible to apply simple electrical systems to the human body.

BARE CONDUCTIVE – ELECTRIC PAINT

Developed at the Royal College of Art in London, the Bare Pen contains the world's first non-toxic, electrically conductive paint that can be applied rather like adhesive glitter. The paint can be used to apply electrical circuits to almost any surface and has been used to equip paper, wood or textiles with electronic systems. The conductive paint can be applied using a pen, and is also available in tubes, cans and screw-top jars. As the paint is non-toxic, it can also be applied to skin, although the manufacturer states that it is not a cosmetically approved product. The paint dries at room temperature and can be removed with soap and water. In addition to accessories for creating lighting systems, the manufacturer also added printable sensors to its product range in 2018.

DuoSkin as an interface
tattoo on the skin
Source: MIT Media Lab;
photo: Jimmy Day

Digital skin as jewellery with
illumination
Source: MIT Media Lab;
photo: Jimmy Day

INTERFACE TATTOO

Scientists at MIT have developed a removable tattoo that can be used to control mobile devices such as smartphones or iPads. Under the name "DuoSkin" the researchers have created a manufacturing process that makes it possible to create individual, functional tattoos. Unlike conventional wearables, the conductive material – available in silver and gold – is applied directly to the skin, much like peel-off tattoos. In combination with integrated LEDs, it is possible to create unusual designs. Wafer-thin gold leaf foil serves as the base material and is inexpensive, skin-friendly and robust enough to withstand everyday use. To transmit control signals, the researchers use an Arduino board connected to the tattoo via thin wires.

Woven textile exoskeleton supporting muscle movements
Source: Thor Balkhed / Linköping University

WOVEN TEXTILE MUSCLES USING ELECTROACTIVE MATERIALS

Researchers at the Universities of Linköping and Borås in Sweden have developed clothing that can assist the wearer by supporting their musculoskeletal system. The concept employs a textile that responds to minimal electrical impulses and contracts and relaxes like a muscle. The scientists' vision is that woven muscles will in future make it easier for handicapped people to go about daily life.

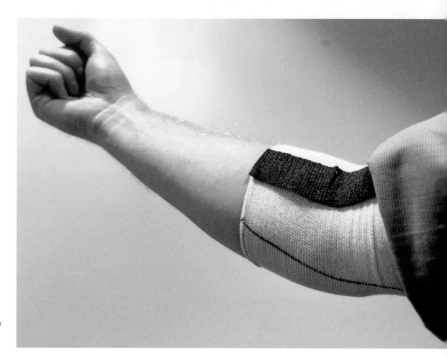

Knitted textile actuator with electrical and mechanical contacts made of copper strip
Source: Thor Balkhed / Linköping University

Technical advances in robotics have given rise to a large number of highly innovative applications in recent years, particularly in the medical sector. Doctors have already succeeded in helping patients who are partially paralysed below the hip to walk again with the help of exoskeletons. However, as the Swedish researchers note, this technology inspired by insect exoskeletons comes with some significant disadvantages: it is bulky, results in unnaturally stiff motion and is extremely costly to produce. Their approach instead focuses on developing a flexible exoskeleton made of textile materials that patients will in future be able to wear under their normal clothing.

The basis of this innovation is a cellulose yarn coated with polypyrrole, a plastic that is flexible and also electroactive. Applying a low voltage to the yarn causes its length and volume to increase. Using different weaving patterns, the researchers can control the properties of a textile to simulate different muscle groups. When the fibres are arranged in a parallel weave, it is even possible to lift small weights.

A further advantage of such fibre coatings is their low production costs. Textile muscles can potentially be mass-produced using conventional production facilities. It is only a matter of time before sportswear manufacturers pick up the technology. In future, sporting competitions may need to introduce "doping rules" that prohibit the wearing of "super textiles".

Gripping technology for robots with electrostatic fingertips
Photo: EPFL/Alain Herzog

GRIPPER SYSTEMS USING ELECTRO-ADHESION

Electro-adhesion is an electrostatic effect between two surfaces which causes temporary adhesion when an electrical voltage is applied. In the context of robotics, it has recently been used for a number of new developments. In 2016, scientists at the École Polytechnique Fédérale de Lausanne (EPFL) developed a gripping system made of stretchable silicone that adapts to the contours of different objects and is capable of safely lifting and moving even fragile objects through electro-adhesion.

Comparable in precision to an index finger and thumb, the two wing-like ends of the system flexibly encompass the contour of an object. The wings consist of five different material layers, a pre-stressed elastomer layer between two electrodes and silicone cover layers. When at rest, the two ends turn slightly upwards, but when a voltage is applied, forces are generated in the electrodes that unroll the tips of the wings so that they curve towards the object like artificial muscles. Electrostatic fields are generated at the tips of the electrodes, which capture the object by electro-adhesion. This approach allows the gripper system to transport up to 100 times its own weight and adapt to different-shaped objects. Foils and paper can be transported as well as food, for example an uncooked egg. When the electrical voltage is switched off, the transported objects can be discharged by the gripper system without leaving any traces.

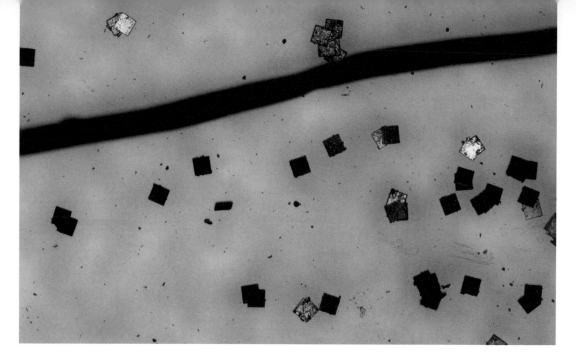

RFID chip next to a human
hair
Source: Hitachi

SMART DUST

"Smart dust" is a pioneering field of technology that is expected to see major innovations and new potential applications over the coming years. The term refers to systems of minute particles with intelligent materials, sensors and microprocessors that are barely noticeable in the environment and can perform useful functions. These "intelligent grains of dust" have the capacity to link the achievements of artificial intelligence, robotics and nanotechnology with the ideas of the Internet of Things

Equipped with controllable mirrors and a self-sufficient power supply, smart dust particles could potentially transmit optical signals and thus data. Through the addition of microsensors, sensor networks could be created for use in dangerous environments, for example to determine data such as temperature or pressure differences in production situations or in disaster areas, such as forest fires, or for medical purposes, and then to transmit them by radio.

Michigan Micro Mote
mini-computer
Source: University of Michigan;
photo: Martin Vloet

Several companies and research institutes have recently been working intensively on the first Smart Dust solutions. Microsensor systems, for example, are already being trialled for recording pressure differences in the brain after head injuries or monitoring intraocular pressure in glaucoma patients. Hitachi has introduced a chip with an edge length of 0.3 mm that is equipped with microelectromechanical system (MEMS) components and can be used as passive RFID tags for the identification and tracking of goods and systems as well as living beings. Under the name "Michigan Micro Mote", the University of Michigan is working on miniature computers that are less than half a centimetre long. A solution measuring 2 × 4 × 4 mm is currently the world's smallest computer and can be seen at the Computer History Museum in California.

ADDITIVE PRODUCTION AND 3D PRINTING

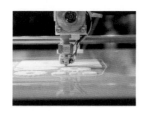

3D printing with bio-based printing material
Source: BIOPRO Baden-Württemberg GmbH

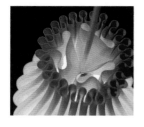

"IDA" – 3D-printed lamp-shade made with a wood-fibre filament
Design: rutan GmbH

The market that has arisen around additive production has grown rapidly in recent years, expanding on average at annual rates of between 25 % and 30 %. One reason lies in the expiration of patent rights for key important processes, such as filament printing in 2009 or laser sintering in 2014, and another in the fact that more and more industries are discovering the advantages of additive manufacturing processes. In combination with the digitalisation of design, purchasing and logistics processes, additive production principles offer excellent potential for making production more flexible, right down to single item production batches. Consequently, additive manufacturing processes are increasingly competing with conventional production techniques such as investment casting, turning or milling. In some product sectors they are even replacing established processes and disrupting the market.

For designers producing their own goods or start-ups with business concepts that redefine the system of trade, production and logistics, the combination of additive production and digital networking opens up new patterns of value creation that place greater emphasis on the product idea, design and construction. 3D printers make it possible to manufacture products with complex geometric forms, undercuts and cavities, or even moving components that cannot be made by conventional means.

Through the expansion into new application areas for additive production and the increasing availability of 3D printers on the market, the range of materials and material combinations that one can now work with has expanded enormously. 3D printing

Cellular Loop – the world's first 3D-printed cantilever chair
Design: Anke Bernotat

3D Housing 05 – bathroom within Europe's first 3D-printed house
Photo: Haute Innovation

4D-printed model for a shape-changing facade structure
Source: ICD/University of Stuttgart

filaments based on natural materials such as algae, lignin or wood fibres are now available, as are filaments with smart qualities such as photoluminescence or retro-reflective properties. Additive production methods can now be used with glass, or for making components and seals made of silicone, which until recently seemed impossible. Similarly, the 3D printing of electrical circuits and permanent magnets offers great potential for the electronics sector.

Through new material developments, additive production processes are currently finding their way into architecture, fashion and furniture construction. The world's first 3D-printed cantilever chair, called "Cellular Loop", was designed by Anke Bernotat. The systems developed by designers have greatly expanded the possibilities for furniture production. The same is true for the field of architecture, where we are also beginning to see successful projects emerging in Europe after the first 3D-printed buildings in China and the Middle East. The first 3D-printed concrete pedestrian bridge was made in Spain and, in April 2018, the first printed house in Europe was completed on the Piazza Cesare Beccaria in Milan. The successful additive production of a metal bridge in Amsterdam has been announced for 2019.

Meanwhile, architects and designers at MIT Media Lab in the USA have made significant advances in developing 4D printing for shape-changing product geometries. Scientists in Stuttgart are currently also exploring the potential of 4D printing for applications in facade construction. And in the food sector, new ways of using food printers are enriching the culinary experience. The possibility of using 3D printers to produce foods with a personalised combination of nutrients is currently being discussed in the medical field.

3D printing with BioFila Silk
Source: twoBEars

BIO-BASED PRINTING MATERIALS

For many years, the materials available for extrusion printing were limited to a few thermoplastics. However, with the increasing shift towards natural and bio-based materials in industry, the range of additive production methods has likewise expanded. Developments have been made in both the printing material and the reinforcing fibres and particles. The bioplastic polylactide (PLA) has in recent years advanced to become the new standard material. Further developments have been made with bio-based fibrous materials such as wood and hemp and in improving biodegradability.

LIGNIN FILAMENT

The German start-up twoBEars was one of the first companies to launch a biodegradable filament for 3D printing under the name BioFila, which came onto the market in April 2014. The company chose not to use polymers from the food chain, instead manufacturing filaments based on thermoplastic lignin. The surface texture can be changed by varying the printing temperature.

LayWood wood filament
Photo: Haute Innovation

Printed GrowLay structures
with plants
Source: Kai Parthy

WOOD FILAMENT

One of the first natural fibre filaments to come onto the market was developed by the Cologne innovator Kai Parthy. Under the name "LayWood", he launched a wood filament consisting of 40% wood fibres and a thermoplastic binder. After printing, the components emit a wood-like odour and have a coarse texture. By varying the temperature of the extrusion head, different colours can even be produced – light at 175 °C, dark at 250 °C – which can be used to create the impression of annual rings. In autumn 2018, Parthy launched "GrowLay", a bio-based printing material that can store water, is biodegradable and can serve as a substrate for planting.

Macadamia nuts
Source: University of Sydney

ALGAE FILAMENT

Algix from the USA was one of the first manufacturers to launch a filament consisting of around 20% algae biomass as the reinforcing material and PLA as the matrix. The 3D algae filament has a thickness of 2.895 mm and is printed at temperatures between 175 and 190 °C. Under the name Solaplast, the company also offers thermoformable hybrid materials based on polyethylene (PE), ethylene vinyl acetate (EVA) and the bioplastics polyhydroxyalkanoate (PHA) and thermoplastic starch (TPS).

PRINTING MATERIAL WITH MACADAMIA PARTICLES

The peel and skin of fruits in nature act as a protective enclosure for the valuable core. The shells of nuts serve a similar purpose and also have very good mechanical properties, which makes them ideal for use as an additive for plastics. Since 2016, researchers at the University of Sydney have been working on integrating macadamia nut particles into a printing filament and using them for additive furniture production with a wood-like appearance.

Large print of a wind turbine
blade made of a cellulose
material
Source: Singapore University of
Technology and Design;
photo: Stylianos Dritsas, J.G. Fermart

3D-printed turbine blade in
detail
Source: Singapore University of Technology and Design; photo: Stylianos
Dritsas, J.G. Fermart

PNEUMATIC BIOMATERIALS DEPOSITION

In order to emulate particularly large near-natural structures, a robot arm-mounted
print head for use with liquid media was developed in 2015 at MIT. It can apply print
material simultaneously through six different extruder nozzles. The mixture of water,
cellulose, hydrogel and the biopolymer chitosan ensures the printed result acquires
sufficient stability after drying or curing.

CELLULOSE PRINTING WITH MUSHROOM ADHESIVE

In mid-2018, scientists at Singapore University of Technology and Design succeeded
in printing a wind turbine blade from a custom-developed cellulose material. No
metallic materials or plastics were used. To provide sufficient stability, the researchers
used a microorganism to bind together the loose cellulose fibres. This development
was inspired by fungus-like oomycetes, also known as egg fungi: tiny microorganisms that resemble real fungi or mycelium threads. The microorganism growth was
stimulated by the addition of small amounts of an acid solution. As neither petroleum-based nor other environmentally unfriendly bonding agents are used, the material can be returned to the biological material cycle at the end of its useful lifetime.

3D GLASS PRINTING

Back in 2011, the designer Markus Kayser demonstrated to stunning effect how grains of sand can be transformed layer by layer into objects made of glass by concentrating the sun's rays using his solar sintering plant. However, as the individual grains were melted and sintered together, the surface of the moulded parts was rough and matt. Since then, researchers have been working on generative production processes to create glass-like objects of crystalline brilliance and transparency.

In late 2015, the Mediated Matter Group at MIT presented outstanding research work on the successful additive processing of glass masses. 3D glass printing (3DGP) is similar in approach to filament 3D printing but instead of melting a plastic mass, glass is heated to temperatures in excess of 1,000 °C to produce a viscous melt. The development team incorporated an extruder that can receive and process the glass mass into a furnace. The team created a collection of expressive bowls and vases that produce impressive light reflections.

MICRON3DP

The first 3D printer for the additive production of highly complex glass components was launched by the Israeli company MICRON3DP in early 2017. The system is capable of processing glass at temperatures between 850 °C (viscous glass) and 1,640 °C (liquid glass) using a temperature- and chemical-resistant borosilicate glass developed by the glass specialists Schott. The resulting additively-produced items are impressively thin and can be highly detailed.

SYNTHETIC RESIN WITH NANOPARTICLES OF QUARTZ GLASS

The Karlsruhe Institute of Technology (KIT) presented a stereolithography process using a liquid synthetic resin containing nanoparticles of high-purity quartz glass. The resin is hardened layer by layer by exposure to light. Unexposed material can be removed from the component with a solvent, and any excess liquid printing material remaining in the system can be reused. After the printing process, the resin is expelled by subsequent heat treatment and the printed component results through the sintering of the glass particles.

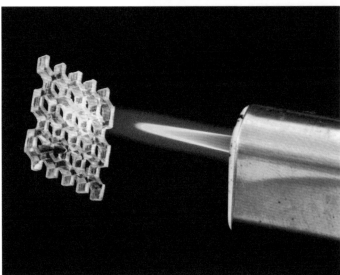

3D-printed glass components
Source: Karlsruhe Institute of Technology KIT

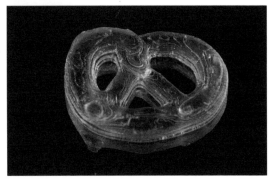

Okkasion – an additive glass
printing process
Source: UdK Berlin

PRINTING PASTES WITH SILICA PARTICLES

A new process has been developed at Lawrence Livermore National Laboratory in the USA for the additive production of glass components at low temperatures: for the 3D printing of so-called compositional glass optics, the scientists created pulp-like printing pastes containing silica particles that can be processed as concentrated suspensions with controllable flow properties at room temperature using direct ink writing (DIW). The printed parts are initially opaque but processing at room temperature makes it possible to achieve the necessary level of detail. The parts are then made transparent by subsequent heat treatment.

OKKASION

At the University of the Arts (UdK) in Berlin, a process chain based on a material mixture of recycled glass and a carrier material was developed to produce glass in an additive 3D printing process. After printing, the carrier material is expelled in a furnace at 900 °C. The recycled glass particles sinter to form the resulting glass element.

3D-printed silicone parts
Source: ACEO, Wacker Chemie

SILICONE PRINTING

Additively produced tube
section made of silicone
elastomer
Source: ACEO, Wacker Chemie

The plastics commonly used for extrusion techniques and laser sintering melt when heat is applied. This was previously not feasible for silicone due to the material's high viscosity.

In 2016, the Wacker chemicals group introduced the first technological solution for the layer-by-layer additive production of objects made of silicone elastomers. The material is applied drop by drop to a building platform with a print head and then vulcanized under UV radiation. The formulations have been carefully perfected so that the silicone droplets flow together before the process of molecular cross-linking sets in. Layer by layer, homogeneous forms with smooth surfaces are created with technical properties comparable to those of standard injection-moulded silicone parts. Their mechanical strength approaches 90-100% of those made with conventional processes, depending on the X, Y and Z dimension. Cavities and overhangs in forms are created with the help of water-soluble support materials.

To process the material, Wacker developed a system with a 3D-guided print head and control software to enable precise portioning and layer-by-layer deposition. The printer works with a voxel size of 0.4mm, making high-precision structures possible. 3D-printed silicone parts can be used for applications in the aerospace, automotive and electro-optical industries and is also intended for producing individualised parts for the sports and medical sectors. Specific applications include spare parts for optical devices, small prosthetic parts or running shoes and insoles tailored to match a person's specific needs. In autumn 2018, Wacker also introduced an electrically conductive elastomeric silicone for additive manufacturing.

A further supplier of printable elastomeric silicones, "Spectroplast", entered the market in summer 2018. The spin-off from the ETH Zurich has developed a process for using commercially available silicones to produce materials for the additive manufacture of components for medical technology applications.

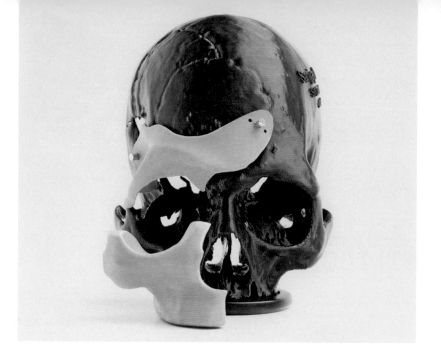

PEEK high-performance
polymer for implants
Source: Apium Additive Technologies

PRINTING MATERIALS
FOR MEDICINE

In medicine, additive production methods are increasingly replacing conventional manufacturing processes for individually-tailored component geometries such as hearing aids, prosthetic devices or dental prostheses. A new field – bioprinting – has emerged for generative manufacturing processes that use tissue engineering techniques to produce human or animal tissue from previously cultivated cells in a bio-ink. Physicians have high hopes for bioprinting: in future, 3D printing of human tissue could, for example, be used to replace skin parts when treating burns, to additively produce entire organs or for the generative production of blood vessels.

BIOCERAMICS FOR 3D-PRINTED BONES

Since 2011, Christine Knabe-Ducheyne, a dentist at Philipps University in Marburg, has been researching new bioceramics for additive production, which she uses to build up collapsed jawbones in order to stimulate growth of the body's own bone structure. The so-called scaffold can be enriched with bone cells and growth hormones and can also contain micro-blood vessels.

3D-printed scaffold
Source: Professor Christine
Knabe-Ducheyne

POLYETHER ETHER KETONE FILAMENT

Apium Additive Technologies based in Karlsruhe has introduced a 3D filament printer for the additive processing of high-performance polymers such as polyetherether-ketone (PEEK) for medical and industrial applications. Due to its specific material qualities, this had previously only been possible to a limited degree. In addition to the printer and the PEEK filament, Apium Additive Technologies has also developed a filament solution using carbon fibres. The resulting filament print can be used in sliding parts in mechanical engineering.

3D PRINTING OF CELLULOSE NANOFIBRILS

Pure cellulose is particularly valuable for medical applications as it is biocompatible and rarely stimulates allergic reactions in the human body. Towards the end of 2015, researchers at Chalmers University of Technology in Gothenburg succeeded for the first time in producing an object from pure cellulose using a bioprinter, a feat that had until then failed because cellulose does not liquefy under the influence of heat. To produce a printable mass, the research team mixed cellulose nanofibrils (CNF) with hydrogel, which is 95-99 % water, for printing using a bioprinter. After printing, the water was removed in a special multi-step freeze-drying process.

3D PRINTING WITH SILK PROTEINS

In South Korea, scientists have successfully developed a 3D printing process for silk proteins for the manufacture of medical implants. As a natural product, silk has exceptional tear resistance but also high elasticity. Science has now been able to produce silk proteins biotechnologically, and additive manufacturing processes would greatly simplify the creation and use of individually customisable and biocompatible silk structures.

ADDITIVE MANUFACTURING
IN THREE-DIMENSIONAL SPACE

The core principle of additive production methods like 3D printing, laser sintering
or fused deposition modelling (FDM) is the application of successive layers of printing material. An object's geometric form is computationally sliced into individual
cross-sections, and the material then applied layer by layer, usually on a building
platform. At present, new methods are attempting to adapt these processes to applying printing material to curved surfaces or to build up objects in three-dimensional
space.

3D PRINTING ON INFLATABLE STRUCTURES

A rather spectacular development in this direction has been undertaken by Fergal
Coulter at Nottingham Trent University in the United Kingdom, who has developed
a process chain for printing onto rotationally symmetrical inflatable structures on
a rotating wheel. Soft silicone is first sprayed onto an air-permeable mandrel. The
resulting membrane is inflated and 3D-scanned to calculate the surface information for the subsequent printing process. Hard silicone is then applied to the inflated
structure using a 3D printing process. This method can be used to produce variable
honeycomb structures with auxetic properties that can be used for medical applications such as artificial muscles or for soft robotics.

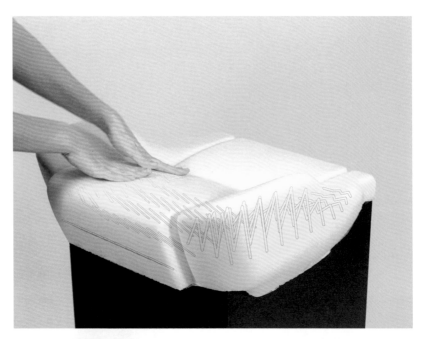

InFoam printing of a foam car seat
Design: Adam Pajonk, Dorothee Clasen, Sascha Praet;
Source: Covestro

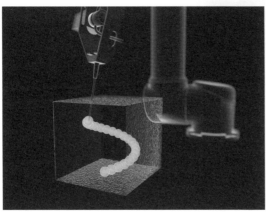

InFoam printing process
Design: Adam Pajonk,
Dorothee Clasen, Sascha Praet;
Source: Covestro

INFOAM PRINTING

As part of an open innovation development project at the chemical company Covestro, the designers Sascha Praet, Dorothee Clasen and Adam Pajonk have developed a 3D printing technology for incorporating structures made of a two-component synthetic polyurethane resin into soft foams. In InFoam Printing, synthetic resin is injected into the foam using a needle-shaped print head, where it cures to form a solid mass. This can be used to partially stiffen localised areas of the foam by injecting the resin in particular geometric configurations. The approach can be used to specifically improve the firmness of upholstered furniture and mattresses. A further application area lies in the design of car seats.

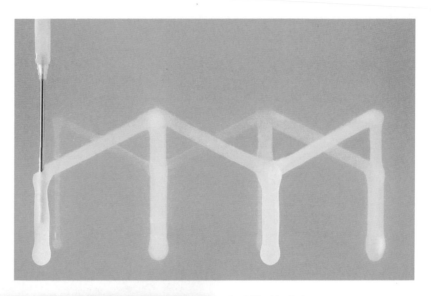

Rapid liquid printing
Source: MIT Self-Assembly Lab,
Christophe Guberan

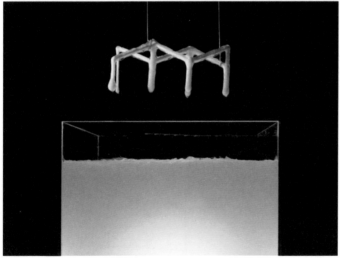

RAPID LIQUID PRINTING

Rapid liquid printing employs a similar approach. Scientists at MIT's Self-Assembly Lab in the USA have used a gel as a supporting material basis for 3D printing in three-dimensional space. The printing material is injected directly into the gel with a needle-shaped print head and reacts there when exposed to UV light. The method was used in a project for a furniture manufacturer to create grid structures as a base for a table top. A second project used this process to produce a three-dimensional handbag.

3D filament Reflect-o-Lay
with retroreflective properties
Source: Kai Parthy

PRINTING MATERIALS WITH SMART PROPERTIES

While just a few years ago the dominant printing filaments for consumer-level 3D printers were based on acrylonitrile-butadiene-styrene copolymers (ABS) or polylactides (PLA), the range of usable printing materials has since expanded considerably. Alongside materials with changing visual characteristics such as fluorescence, photochromism or thermochromism, new exciting printing materials with specific smart properties are emerging.

REFLECT-O-LAY

This patent-protected printing filament contains millions of tiny reflecting pigments that are responsible for the optical effect of retroreflection, a phenomenon familiar from reflective road markings. Without direct light shining on it, the material is a light grey colour, but as soon as it is illuminated, it reflects the light rays back in exactly the same direction from which they come, producing the familiar striking light effect.

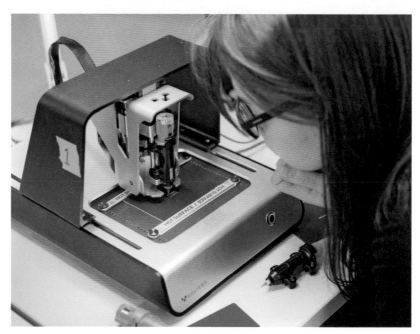

Voltera V-One – PCB printer
for 3D-printed electronic
applications
Source: Voltera

VOLTERA V-ONE

The quick manufacture of printed circuit boards is vital for the product development of digital and medical devices. Voltera V-One is a printer for conductive pastes and insulating inks developed by a team of developers at Waterloo University in Canada. These are printed in two layers so that functional electronic circuits can be produced within a short space of time. The print head can also be used for soldering pastes, making it possible to add further components later in the development process.

3D printing filament with
magnetic qualities
Source: TU Vienna

MAGNETIC FILAMENT

Production technology for the manufacture of permanent magnets with powerful magnetic attraction is currently the state of the art. However, producers still have difficulties when it comes to making magnets with complex geometries and specific desired magnetic fields. In late 2016, scientists at Vienna University of Technology presented a 3D printing filament with magnetic properties, making it possible for the first time to additively produce permanent magnets with tailor-made magnetic fields. The filament consists of a polymer matrix into which a magnetic microgranulate has been mixed. After the printing process, the initially non-magnetic material is exposed to a strong external magnetic field to give the material its permanent magnetism. The effect can be precisely adjusted. Around 90 % of the printed moulded part consists of the magnetic material.

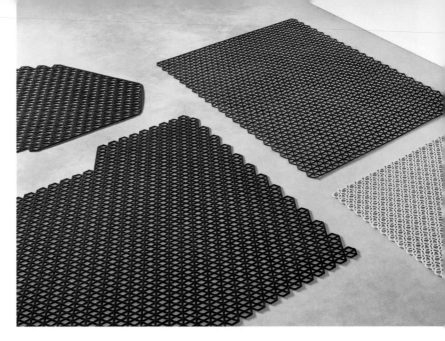

3D-printed rug Open Rugs
with flock coating
Source: Studio Plott

HYBRID ADDITIVE MANUFACTURING PROCESSES

Additive production processes have the potential to significantly transform product and object manufacturing in many different sectors. At present, however, they have been employed to best advantage mainly in combination with traditional manufacturing methods. Having pushed the boundaries of 3D printing in recent years, designers are now turning to ways in which to exploit their potential together with other techniques to create new hybrid production methods.

OPEN RUGS

In spring 2017, the Dutch designers Studio Plott presented the first 3D-printed rugs, the individual geometry and shape of which were designed on a computer. To give the rugs a familiar tactile feel, the additive plastic structures were given a soft flock coating, as often used, for example, on garments.

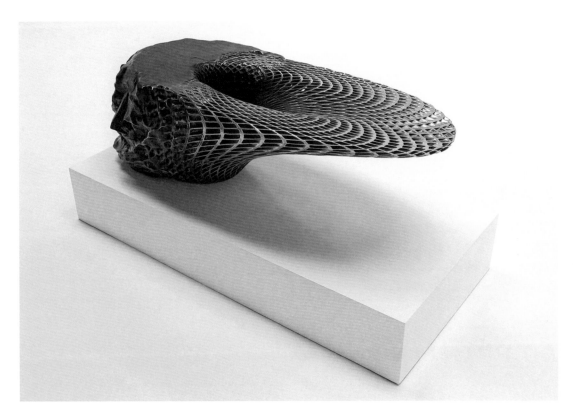

Metsidian table
Source: Janne Kyttanen

FORGEBRID

By combining the two production processes of forging and laser melting, new products can be manufactured quickly even when highly complex. In this advanced process chain, the advantages of forming technology complement the possibilities of additive manufacturing. Solid components with complex cavity structures can be produced cost-effectively, making optimum use of resources.

Solid component made by forging and laser melting
Source: Rosswag

METSIDIAN TABLE

To produce the Metsidian Table out of a combination of copper and volcanic obsidian, the Finnish designer Janne Kyttanen developed a new production process that combines an additive manufacturing process with explosion welding. Explosion welding is most commonly used to join different materials that are weldable only at high temperatures. While the melting point of copper is just below 1,100 °C, volcanic rock melts at temperatures well above 1,400 °C.

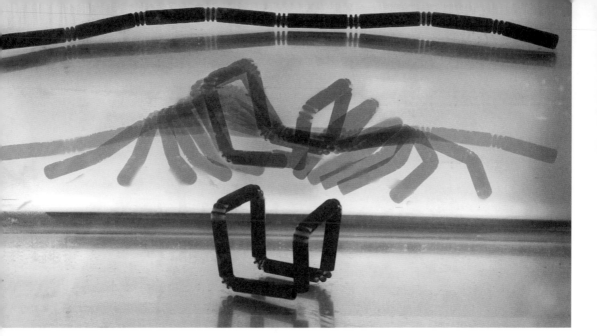

4D printing with a hydrophilic
acrylated monomer
Source: MIT Self Assembly Lab,
Skylar Tibbits

4D PRINTING

4D printing originated at MIT's Self-Assembly Lab in Cambridge, USA, and was first presented as a new technological development in 2013. 4D printing refers to a three-dimensional printing process in which, after additive processing, the printed material can dynamically change shape when actuated by an external impulse, in turn triggering other functions. The external impulse may be triggered by light, magnetic fields, temperature fluctuations or the action of moisture. Research teams at various facilities around the globe are now investigating possible fields and application scenarios for this new technology. In addition to applications in medicine, aviation and architecture, potential uses in the automotive industry as well as the fashion and clothing industry have already been explored.

MOISTURE AND LIGHT-SENSITIVE PRINTING MATERIALS

One of the first research projects in this field at MIT was a hydrophilic acrylated monomer developed by Skylar Tibbits in collaboration with Autodesk for 4D printing. The material cures in a water bath under UV light to form a hydrogel, expanding in volume by up to 50 %. In another development project, light-sensitive printing materials were successfully tested in shape-transforming carbon fibre structures. In vehicle construction, 4D printing could be used to implement shape-changing car body parts.

Mimicking natural plant motion by 4D printing a hydrogel ink and cellulose fibrils
Source: Wyss Institute, Harvard University

HYDROGEL AND CELLULOSE FIBRILS

At Harvard University in the USA, scientists have successfully simulated the natural movement of plant blossoms under the influence of moisture using a hydrogel printing ink and cellulose fibrils. The shape-changing process exploits the exceptional hygroscopic properties of the cellulose fibres: when exposed to moisture, the fibre expands much more in the direction of growth than at right angles to it. After printing the ink in two directions and placing the result in a water bath, the material compound began shortly afterwards to deform, causing the geometry of the moulded part to bend upwards. The scientists used an algorithm specially developed for the specific composition of the printing ink to calculate the form change process.

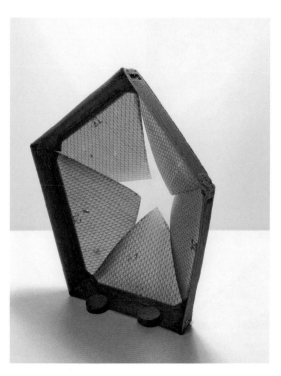

Model of a shape-changing
facade produced by 3D printing using a moisture-sensitive wood filament
Source: ICD, University of Stuttgart

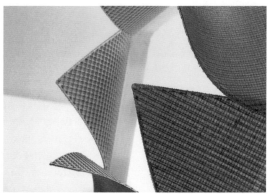

HYGROSCOPIC WOOD PRESSURE FILAMENT

A team of researchers at the University of Stuttgart has used a similar approach to
create a shape-changing architectural structure by 3D printing using the LayWood
wood filament by cc-products in Cologne. In this printing technology, David Correa
and his team exploited the hygroscopic properties of the printing material to cause the
additive structures to react to fluctuations in air humidity. The research team envisages being able to print wooden facade elements that will open when the sun shines
and close automatically when it rains.

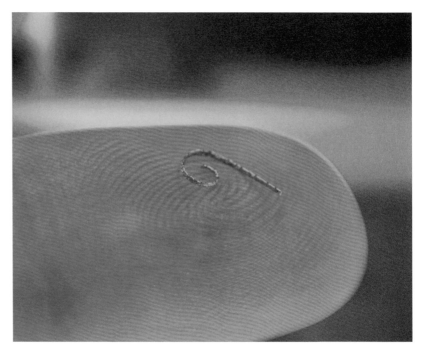

Micro-actuator for cochlear implants produced by laser sintering
Source: Laser Zentrum Hannover LZH

SHAPE MEMORY POLYMER

At Singapore University of Technology and Design, scientists are investigating the potential of 4D printing by integrating fibres from a shape memory polymer into a multi-material assembly for self-expanding systems. Different material combinations were tested, and their mechanical properties correlated against the respective activation temperature.

SHAPE MEMORY ALLOY

At the Laser Zentrum Hannover (LZH), shape memory materials made of a nickel-titanium alloy are used for the additive production of cochlear implants for the deaf by laser sintering a starting material in powder form. The shape-change process is activated by body heat causing the implant to adapt to the individual shape of the cochlea. The scientists are also working on developing a similar effect for implants used in facial surgery.

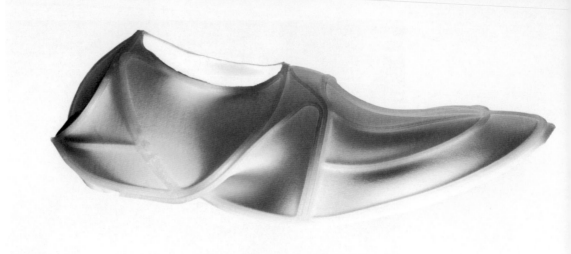

Active Shoe – self-trans-
forming shoe made with 4D
printing
Source: Christophe Guberan, Carlo
Clopath, MIT Self Assembly Lab

4D TEXTILES

4D textiles are two-dimensional textiles that are stretched then printed with a plastic. On release, they independently shape-transform to exhibit a three-dimensional geometry. The change in shape does not require any external energy input as the required energy is already stored within the textile. The fourth dimension in the process is the factor of time.

PROGRAMMABLE TEXTILES

As far back as late 2014, the Self-Assembly Lab at MIT in the USA presented various shape-transforming textile structures under the term "Programmable Textiles", which were created by printing onto a stretched textile. The potential of the technology was investigated for a number of applications, including the shoe and fashion industries. In collaboration with the Swiss designer Christophe Guberan, for example, objects were created for the Life on Foot exhibition by the shoe brand Camper at the London Design Museum. As an example of 4D printing, they created the "Active Shoe" with a self-transforming upper.

4D printing of an exoskeleton
that helps humans to exert a
gripping force
Source: ITA Institute of Textile
Technology, RWTH Aachen

Sonogrid – a printing process
for acoustic damping 4D
textiles
Source: Sascha Praet, Dorothee
Clasen, Oliver Köneke, Moritz
Wallasch

ACOUSTIC DAMPING 4D TEXTILES

Designers in Cologne employed the 4D printing principle to create acoustic 4D textiles. The "sonogrid" material system is designed for reducing acoustic reflections in heavily frequented public spaces. The coarse-mesh fabric is printed in a stretched state and after printing contracts to form a three-dimensional grid of small pyramids. The size and orientation of these pyramids can be adapted to meet the optimum noise reduction needs of different spaces.

4D TEXTILES FOR EXOSKELETONS

A research team at RWTH Aachen University is working on applications of 4D textiles for medical technology. For example, an exoskeleton was created by printing a pre-stressed textile with a polymer so that the energy stored within the textile helps stimulate and facilitate the flow of various movements for the wearer.

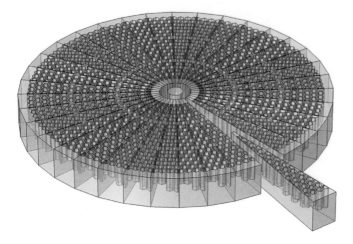

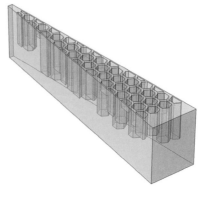

The 20 cm radius structure of the metamaterial multi-speaker listener and one fan-shaped waveguide
Source: Duke University

3D-PRINTED METAMATERIALS

The class of metamaterials refers to substances with extraordinary properties that do not occur naturally in this form. The most well-known effect is the negative refraction of light, which makes an object appear invisible, because the material deflects light waves around it. In future, scientists hope to use additive manufacturing techniques not only to develop metamaterials with outstanding qualities, but also to employ them directly in the manufacture of products.

ACOUSTIC METAMATERIAL FOR LOCALISING NOISE SOURCES

In Durham, North Carolina, a 3D-printed disc shape with a complex internal geometry was developed that can channel and distinguish sounds and voices from up to 36 noise sources for recording with a computer. The structure of the disc influencing the sound is smaller than the wavelength of the acoustic waves.

3D-printed cells for a door
latch with metamaterial
mechanism
Source: Hasso Plattner Institute/
Alexandra Ion

MODULAR ACOUSTIC METAMATERIAL
FOR TREATING TUMOURS

Scientists from Sussex, England, have demonstrated that acoustic metamaterials can also be used in the medical sector by 3D printing cuboid structures that can more effectively focus ultrasound waves for treating tumour tissue. The result was 16 different "bricks" with a height of 8.66 mm, an edge length of 4.33 mm and an undulating inner structure that can influence a phase shift of the ultrasound waves in the range of 0 and 2π in order to generate any acoustic field necessary for treatment purposes.

METAMATERIAL MECHANISMS

By producing a geometry with a special arrangement of "shear cells", scientists at the Hasso Plattner Institute in Potsdam have succeeded in producing a door handle without screws, springs or bolts. The 3D-printed cells transmit mechanical stress by buckling, bending and folding, in the process converting a rotary motion into a linear motion. The bolt is drawn back so that the door can open. Once the handle is released, the cells return to their original shape.

Printed sugar sculptures
Source: 3D Systems

FOOD PRINTERS

One of the most unusual applications for 3D printers is undoubtedly the food industry. Food printers have been used both to create spectacular culinary experiences and for providing foodstuffs with personalised nutritional content to the medical sector. In future it will be possible to add specific substances, such as omega-3 fatty acids, to food and to create food for consumption from sustainable sources of calories. In the meantime, food printers for the production of pasta, individually customisable baked goods, cakes and filled chocolates have appeared on the market as have food printers for fruit gums, marzipan, chocolate and sculptures made of sugar.

CHEFJET

3D Systems, one of the large system manufacturers of 3D printers, launched its first products for the emerging food printing market in 2013. The pioneering 3D printer firm took over Sugar Lab in Los Angeles after it caused a sensation with a large exhibition of 3D-printed sugar sculptures. Using a colour jet printer, a designer and an architect created edible shapes from natural binders and powdered sugar. Since then, 3D Systems has successfully launched a commercial food printer called "ChefJet" for creating special culinary experiences in restaurants and pastry shops.

Foodini pizza printer
Source: Natural Machines

3D-printed chocolate
Source: Choc Edge, UK

FOODINI PIZZA PRINTER

Natural Machines, a start-up from Barcelona, launched the first pizza printer under the name "Foodini". This printer not only bakes the pizza but can also print any food-stuffs made of a pasty mass or where the ingredients need to be melted under heat. In addition to pizza, the Foodini can also produce dishes made of minced meat, baked goods such as cakes or biscuits and recipes made of chocolate. All ingredients are pre-prepared for 3D printing in heatable metal cylindrical capsules and applied by the machine with a syringe.

CHOC EDGE CHOCOLATE PRINTER

The Choc Edge Choc Creator is a 3D chocolate printer. The device is intended for choco-latiers, confectioners and restaurants and the company envisages that we will start to see special chocolate shops in our cities where customers can print out chocolate sculptures in designs of their own making.

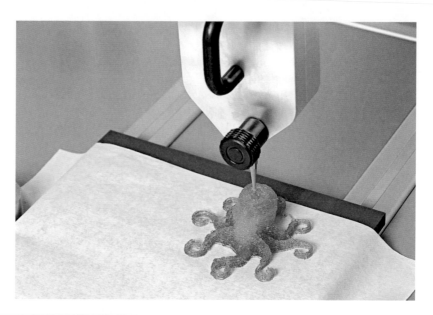

3D candy printer
Source: Katjes Magic Candy Factory

3D-printed pasta delicacies
Source: TNO, Delft

PASTA PRINTER

In cooperation with the Dutch research institute TNO in Delft, the Italian food manufacturer Barilla has developed a 3D printer for pasta. Much like modern coffee machines, this printer works with cartridges containing dough mixtures of durum wheat flour and water. The printer can be used to produce pasta in customisable shapes and compositions. The company aims to print a plate of pasta in two minutes. More recently, research has intensified into developing printable, gluten-free noodles made from wholegrain and vegetables.

FRUIT GUM PRINTER

The world's first fruit gum printer, the Magic Candy Factory, was launched at Katjes Café Grün-Ohr in Berlin in late 2015. Customers could choose between eight flavours and the corresponding colours and designs could be created from combinations of up to ten different basic shapes. Each fruit gum, weighing up to 20g, could be made from a choice of vegan, lactose-free or gluten-free ingredients. Depending on the shape and ingredient, the printing process took between one and five minutes.

Print a Drink
Source: Benjamin Greimel, Philipp Hornung, Johannes Braumann; Photo: Philipp Moosbrugger

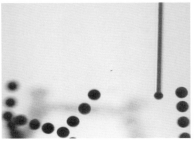

PRINT A DRINK

As part of Pioneers Challenge 2017, the world's first 3D printing technology for liquid foods and beverages was awarded one of the 3D Pioneers Challenge Prizes. The print head uses a robotic arm to place drops of oil into a host beverage. In the context of today's trend-setting molecular gastronomy, the printer makes it possible to produce stunning individual 3D cocktail creations.

3D-printed office building
in Dubai
Photo: Haute Innovation

3D Housing 05 – the first
3D-printed house in Europe
Photo: Haute Innovation

3D PRINTERS IN ARCHITECTURE

As early as 2002, the concept of "Contour Crafting" was discussed as a means of using generative manufacturing processes for architecture. After nearly a decade of exploration and research, more and more model projects have begun to emerge since 2012. With the increase in size and range of additive printing systems, the development of new materials and the ability to use robot-guided systems in construction contexts came a surge in innovation that has made additive manufacture an increasingly feasible proposition in the construction sector. In May 2016, the first 3D-printed office building was opened in Dubai and the first 3D-printed concrete pedestrian bridge was produced in Spain. As part of Milan Design Week 2018, a consortium of companies built the first 3D-printed house in Europe on Piazza Cesare Beccaria near Milan Cathedral.

190

3D-printed concrete
component made of cement-
bonded material
Source: Asko Fromm

3D-printed concrete structure
with steel reinforcement
Source: Imprimere

BIG 3D CONCRETE PRINTING USING PASTE EXTRUSION

Imprimere AG from Switzerland presented the first fully functional system in Europe at the Hanover Trade Fair in April 2015. The large-format printer with a portal frame design has maximum dimensions of 5.75 × 6.00 × 6.25 m and can produce additive concrete components to an accuracy of 0.5 mm after milling. The robot inserts any required reinforcement between the layers at defined intervals in order to achieve the specified structural requirements for load-bearing elements of the building. The portal printer can be used to produce curved building elements such as spiral staircases, large-dimension furniture or facade elements, as well as free-form parts, sculptures or an entire building with several storeys made of concrete.

3D PRINTING OF CEMENT-BONDED COMPONENTS

Most additive production processes for building components require the mixing of a uniform paste of liquid and cement powder before the actual printing process can begin. Asko Fromm has developed a 3D printing process at the University of Kassel for the production of high-precision concrete components in which a cement material is mixed with aggregates and applied in layers using a voxeljet printer. Selective binding by the application of an aqueous solution layer by layer causes the required parts of the component to harden and gain strength. The mixture can also be selectively stabilised layer by layer using an aqueous solution.

3D-printed metal bridge
Source: MX3D

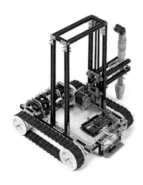

Minibuilders
Source: IAAC Barcelona, Saša Jokić

MINIBUILDERS

In 2014, a research team at the Institute for Advanced Architecture (IAAC) in Barcelona led by Saša Jokić and Petr Novikov presented a family of small construction robots that can be used to print building materials that harden hydraulically. The aim was to design a series of different-sized robotic systems that can independently perform a variety of tasks in the various construction phases. Each robot is equipped with sensors and a positioning system to record live data and to coordinate the systems using central control software. The robots are supplied with printing material via pipes and hoses from a supply robot.

ROBOT-GUIDED METAL DEPOSITION WELDING PROCESS

Since 2015, Joris Laarman and his company MX3D have been working on a robot-guided metal deposition welding technique for the additive manufacture of a metal bridge. The process uses commercially available welding rod, which is melted and applied in layers. The speed of the system had to be carefully adjusted to ensure the printed part hardened sufficiently fast to avoid the need for supporting structures for undercuts and overhangs. The 3D-printed metal bridge was produced in 2018 and is due to be installed in Amsterdam in 2019.

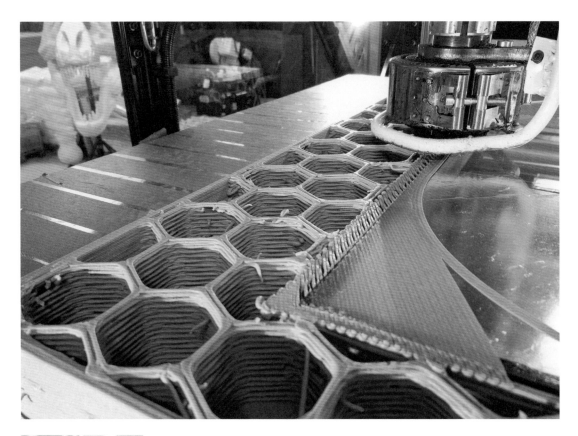

10 SMARTA KVADRAT

The Swedish start-up BLB Industries presented a large-scale printer for plastic components that employs fused granular fabrication (FGF) technology and is currently one of the largest 3D plastic printers in the world. In cooperation with a Swedish construction company, the BLB printer produced a wall unit with a recessed window under the name "10 Smarta Kvadrat", made of PLA bioplastic with 20% wood fibre. The wall unit is a demonstration of the construction plant's capacity to create affordable living accommodation. With a nozzle diameter of 2 mm, the large-scale printer took around a week to produce the ten components.

10 Smarta Kvadrat – 3D printing of a wall structure using BLB large-format printers
Source: BLB Industries

7

INTELLIGENT SYSTEMS AND BIO-INSPIRED SURFACES

UPANDDOWN combines wool and nickel-titanium alloys, two seemingly contradict-ory low- and high-tech materials, to create a lifestyle product
Source: Laura Risch, smart³ research initiative

If the predictions of materials experts come to pass, we will see a shift over the next 20 years from products that are highly complex constructions to those equipped with material intelligence. Until recently, products that fulfilled a variety of functions usually required a large number of components. In future, however, the ability to endow materials or material surfaces with functionality will lead to greater structural simplicity.

Materials that change shape when heated, that react to changes in air humidity or can change shape from one stable geometric form to another are called "smart materials" and are predicted to unlock great potential in the coming years. In architecture in particular, as well as in vehicle manufacturing, the incorporation of functions into a material has the potential, according to experts, to reduce to a minimum the resources required to realise complex mechanisms. After a decade of explorative research into the underlying mechanisms of smart materials, researchers and companies are now introducing promising products that open up new market applications and give designers much greater design freedom.

In addition, science is increasingly drawing inspiration from nature for intelligent solutions, which when transferred and applied to technology have the potential to be of considerable value. One such example is the so-called Salvinia effect, which can be found in some animals and plants such as floating ferns, from which it derives its name. When immersed in water, the highly water-repellent, superhydrophobic

194

surface causes a static layer of air to form that has a friction-reducing effect. When applied to shipbuilding, this effect could reduce energy consumption considerably.

One of the most spectacular recent developments is the ability to give natural materials and organic structures magnetic, electrically conductive or even luminous properties. Scientists at MIT in the USA, for example, reported in mid-2017 on the success of an experiment in which nanoparticles were embedded in living watercress leaves, causing them to glow yellow-green for a few hours. What seemed like science fiction just a few years ago is slowly becoming reality through the use of smart material technologies. The scientists in the US are already dreaming of avenues in which luminous trees can serve as street lighting.

HygroSkin Pavilion with
moisture-sensitive flaps
Source: Professor Achim Menges,
ICD/University of Stuttgart

Progress on the development of materials with self-healing properties is at a similar level. Many product developers, architects and designers are eagerly awaiting a successful breakthrough in these experiments. Scientists recently presented solutions in which the self-healing process also occurs in materials that have been mechanically sliced in two and then re-joined.

MULTI-STABLE FIBRE
COMPOSITE STRUCTURES

Material composites that are structurally stable in several geometric states are proving increasingly useful in a variety of industrial fields. Their ability to change quickly between different stable geometric shapes offers particular potential for applications in aircraft construction, in defence and military contexts, for specific energy systems as well as in the context of temporary structures.

ROLATUBE

A British company has launched a fibre-reinforced composite structure under the name "RolaTube" that is sold wound in reels but transforms into a stable tubular form when unrolled. Its bi-stable properties can be attributed to the special arrangement of fibre structures in the thermoplastic matrix. After use, the tubular elements can be easily rolled up back into a reel. The system can be used in temperatures ranging from –150 to +250 °C, is particularly lightweight and acquires considerable strength with very little material input. Mast systems up to a height of 8 m and a weight of 16 kg can be erected in less than 5 minutes. Tripod solutions are also available for quickly erecting temporary structures or for use as supports for a mobile solar panel array.

The object is printed flat (left) and can subsequently be transformed into two other stable, load-bearing shapes (centre and right)
Source: ETH Zurich, Tian Chen

3D-PRINTED LIFTING ELEMENT

A research group at the ETH Zurich is investigating how a 3D-printed assembly made of a multi-material structure using a shape-memory polymer can be used to convert flat kits into various stable load-bearing object geometries when heated. The focus of the investigation is a lifting element that changes between two possible states – collapsed or expanded, although structures with several stable positions are also conceivable. Using software, the scientists hope to be able to accurately predict the change in shape.

3D AUXETICS

A weaving loom for making auxetic structures

If a material becomes thicker when stretched and thinner when compressed, it most likely has an auxetic structure. This unusual behaviour is the product of a simple geometric structure. While most research up to now has explored two-dimensional auxetic structures, the first applications of 3D auxetics are currently under development.

Auxetic structures and materials exhibit atypical deformation behaviour. When pulled apart, cavities form within the material, increasing its volume but decreasing its density. Physicists describe this phenomenon with the help of a measure of material stability called the Poisson's ratio. If the ratio is positive, the material behaves much as one would expect. Cork, for example, has a Poisson's ratio approaching 0.0, while that of rubber is already 0.5. Due to their specific inner structure, auxetic materials have a negative Poisson's ratio which can be as much as -1. The particular mechanical properties of auxetic materials, their resistance to breaking and high energy capacity mean that auxetic fibres or foams are particularly suitable for safety applications or for use in shock, impact or sound absorbers.

3D-PRINTED AUXETIC STRUCTURES

For his thesis at the Royal College of Art in London, the designer Oluwaseyi Sosanya presented a loom that can create three-dimensional auxetic structures. Similar to 3D printing, the structures are built up in layers. The starting material, however, is not a plastic filament that bonds to itself, it is yarn. A weaving head controlled by program control code moves the yarn around metal tubes fixed vertically on the pick-up table and produces a hexagonal scrim with auxetic properties. These allow the textile structure to withstand impacts of more than 300 g and are particularly suitable for buffering recurring external loads. The zigzag weave is lightweight and extremely flexible and therefore ideally suited to applications in medical technology as well as in the automotive and sportswear industries.

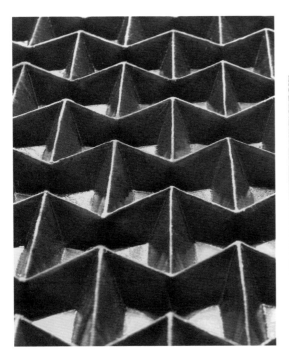

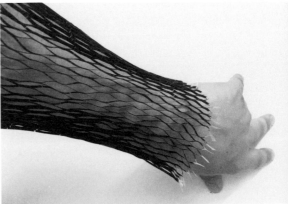

Active Auxetic – an auxetic material that behaves like the pores of human skin
Source: MIT Self Assembly Lab

Panel material with auxetic properties
Source: Pietsch & Partner

PANELS WITH AN AUXETIC STRUCTURE

A process for the production of three-dimensional auxetic structures was patented in Wismar, Germany, for use in aviation applications, vehicle construction, architecture and design. By embossing and folding a flat semi-finished product, geometries with auxetic properties, networks of channels and honeycomb chambers can be produced. Due to their specific cellular structure, the lightweight panels can be interlocked without the need for a binder and can therefore join together to form large surfaces interlinking the various functions. With appropriate coatings, functions can be incorporated that range from data, power, energy and heat transmission and retention to sensor technologies.

ACTIVE AUXETIC

In 2017, scientists from the renowned MIT in the USA presented an active auxetic material that behaves like the pores of human skin. It can react to external stimuli such as temperature fluctuations and increased UV radiation. In cold temperatures, it contracts to retain heat inside the body, relaxing again as the temperature rises. The type and dimension of deformation is individually programmable. The idea is to develop a smart, all-in-one garment that, like skin, can react to environmental conditions.

THERMAL MEMORY MATERIALS

Thermal memory materials are mostly metallic or polymeric shape memory materials that change their geometric shape when an activation temperature is reached. In metals, the effect is a product of different crystalline structures in which a shape memory alloy can occur in both stable states. When a specific temperature is reached, a lattice transformation within the crystalline structure produces a change in shape. The transformation only occurs within certain narrow temperature ranges and cannot be adjusted freely. Some materials have a one-way memory effect, while others can return to their original form when the temperature change is reversed (two-way memory effect). Thermal memory materials are most widely used in medical technology, for example in stents, or in the automotive industry.

As part of the "smart³" research initiative headed by the Fraunhofer Institute for Machine Tools and Forming Technology (IWU) in Dresden, new product scenarios for shape memory materials have been developed since 2013. These range from self-regulating sun-shading systems for architecture to approaches for improving the efficiency of electric drives for use in vehicles. Shape memory materials based on plastics are also being developed, including some interesting applications of shape memory foams in packaging and in space travel.

SMART CUSHION TO PREVENT CRANIAL DEFORMATION

Almost 20 % of all new-born babies around the world are affected by cranial deformation because they sleep predominantly on their backs at night. Cumulino is an active support cushion designed by Lukas Boxberger at Burg Giebichenstein in Halle, Germany, that prevents skull asymmetries in infancy and employs the functionality of thermal shape memory alloys. The child's head is shifted gently from left to right and back again without interrupting sleep by slowly and silently changing the shape of the cushion. Shape memory actuators are integrated into a flexible plastic matrix inside the cushion and prevent the baby's head from resting on one side only.

The Cumulino pillow moves
a child's head silently and
gently into different positions
Source: Fraunhofer IWU

As the integral shape memory actuators of the Solar Curtain warm up, they cause the flower-like petals of the sun shade to open and shield the interior from direct sunlight
Source: smart³ research initiative

The Solar Curtain uses the sun's energy to shade glass facades
Source: Fraunhofer IWU & Weißensee Kunsthochschule Berlin

The shape memory actuators of the UPANDDOWN demonstrator are incorporated into the wool structure and respond to the heat of the sun, causing the blind to open independently
Source: Laura Risch, smart³ research initiative

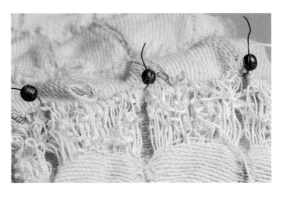

SOLAR CURTAIN

Together with scientists at the Fraunhofer IWU, the textile designer Bára Finnsdottir has developed a blackout system consisting of 72 flower-like structures at the Kunsthochschule Berlin-Weissensee. Each individual element of the solar curtain incorporates an 80-mm-long shape memory actuator that activates the opening and closing mechanism. As the facade warms up in the sunshine, the nickel-titanium alloy wires deform and contract when they reach a certain activation temperature. The flowers then open, covering the facade and shading the interior from the sun. When the temperature drops in the evening, the process reverses allowing light to shine on the facade. Another shading system, designed by Laura Risch, combines wool and nickel-titanium shape memory alloys.

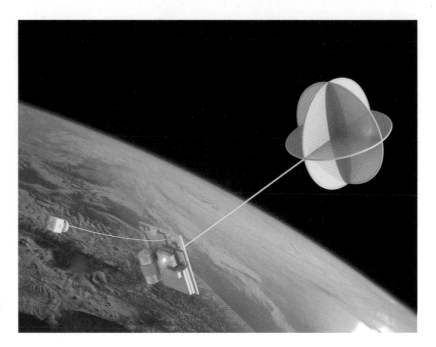

ThumbSat – a self-deploying
satellite
Source: Noumenon

SELF-DEPLOYING SATELLITE

Under the name "ThumbSat", a satellite-like space station is currently being built for undertaking experiments in space but without the vast cost investments usually required. The idea of the project is to give small research teams access to university research in space as well as to undertake larger projects. After a lifetime of 8 to 12 weeks, the satellite disintegrates in the extreme conditions of space, leaving behind no waste. In order to transport the development platform into space in a compact form, a polyurethane-based shape memory foam will be used that is currently being developed at Noumenon in Belgrade. The material can be compressed for transport purposes to minimise its volume. When it reaches its intended destination, the foam regains its original shape by heating to an activation temperature and the ThumbSat then automatically unfolds into a pre-defined position.

Breathing facade made
of thousands of laser-cut
bimetal strips
Source: Doris Kim Sung

BREATHING SYSTEMS

Many attempts have been made to transfer the pattern of human breathing to buildings and vehicles, not just to improve their functionality but also to integrate them
visually into their surroundings. Some impressive examples show how the innovative
use of materials in combination with smart control technology and automation can
bring developers closer to their goals.

BREATHING FACADE

An architectural example is the Breathing Metal Wall by Doris Kim Sung. It consists
of thousands of laser-cut bimetal strips that bend in one direction when heated, for
example when the sun shines, due to the different coefficients of expansion of the two
metals. The resulting openings in the facade can be used for air conditioning.

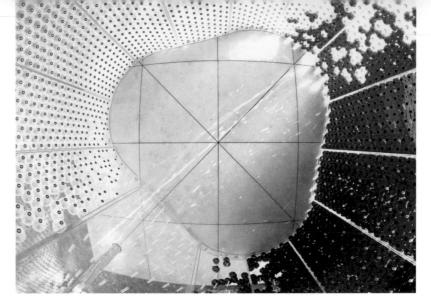

Breathing Skins
Source: Tobias Becker

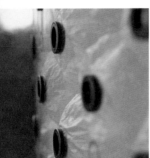 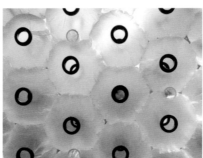

BREATHING SKINS

Tobias Becker pursued a similar goal at the University of Stuttgart with Breathing Skins, developed in cooperation with Festo. The system's main component is a pneumatic muscle that is activated by changes in air pressure and can be either open or closed. These elements respond to environmental influences such as air pressure, sound, temperature and incidence of light, adapting accordingly so that the energy requirements of buildings can be significantly reduced.

CONCEPT BREATHE

The "Concept Breathe" study by the car manufacturer AUDI re-imagines the car seat as a breathing organism. Under the direction of Manuel Kretzer, a development team at Braunschweig University of Fine Arts (HBK) has developed a car seat that represents an innovative vision of a dynamic component for tomorrow's autonomous vehicles. To dynamically adapt its visual and tactile properties, 38 customised, active components were developed and integrated into the seat's surface. These enable the seat to alter its shape in response to changing driving conditions and help users to identify with the vehicle through breathing movements.

"Concept Breathe" study for
a car seat
Source: HBK Braunschweig

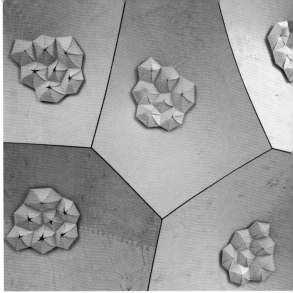

HygroSkin Pavilion with
1,100 moisture-sensitive
flaps
Source: Professor Achim Menges,
ICD/University of Stuttgart

HYGROSCOPIC SHAPE-CHANGING MATERIALS

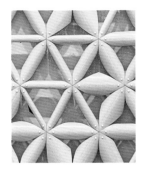

Water-reactive architectural
surface
Source: Chao Chen

That materials can change shape in response to moisture has been demonstrated impressively by Achim Menges' HygroSkin Pavilion at the University of Stuttgart and the water-reactive facade element developed by the product designer Chao Chen at the Royal College of Art in London. Both developments draw their inspiration from the natural model of the pinecone, which closes tightly when wet or humid and re-opens when dry, revealing its structure. This principle can serve as a model for climate-adaptive architecture.

Both projects employ thin and originally flat plywood, which automatically furls and unfurls in response to changes in air humidity, revealing openings in the skin of the building. The effect exploits the hygroscopic properties of wood: cellulose fibres bind water molecules in the fibre structure as the ambient humidity rises, resulting in a change in volume, which in many wood species is greater in the direction of fibre growth than across it. By controlling the direction of the fibres in the thin layers of wood and firmly bonding the layers to one another, the different directions of expansion of the fibres create a tension that produces a cupping effect in the wood, causing the individual elements to bend.

The HygroSkin Pavilion comprises 28 individual facade panels, into which a total of 1,100 moisture-sensitive flaps have been embedded. The flaps open and close independently in response to humidity changes, ranging from 30% (sunny day) to 90% (rainy day), and require neither an external energy source nor expensive electronics.

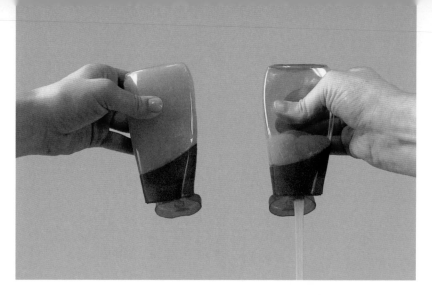

LiquiGlide technology for permanently wet and slippery surfaces
Source: LiquiGlide Inc.

PERMANENTLY LIQUID-IMPREGNATED SURFACES

LiquiGlide is the only company in the world to produce a permanently wet and slippery surface, a property that is useful, for example, for pressing viscous masses out of a tube or for creating water-repellent surfaces. The product derives from developments at MIT in the USA, and the patented concept is now commercially marketed by the start-up LiquiGlide, also based in Cambridge, MA. The technology already serves as a basis for a large number of customer-specific, impregnated coatings.

LiquiGlide differs from conventional superhydrophobic surfaces in that instead of trapping a cushion of air within a highly-textured surface over which water droplets roll, as seen in the "Lotus effect", it provides a permanently liquid-impregnated surface, so that water droplets roll away over a layer of liquid. The principle employs a multi-layer system comprising a solid, highly-textured surface and a layer of liquid held in place within the texture, resulting in a permanently wet liquid surface.

Applications include improving the flow of liquid and viscous foodstuffs from bottles and tubes to help reduce food waste, preventing blockages in gas and oil pipelines or improving work processes in industry and crafts. The technology has now been perfected to such a degree that it is possible to precisely adjust the rate at which liquids run off a surface.

ANTI-ICING SURFACES

Ice can have a very detrimental effect in the energy and mobility sectors and in aviation and can even lead to the stoppage or failure of entire systems. For example, wind turbines have to be switched off in winter when frozen, and the wings of aircraft have to be de-iced before take-off, often with the use of copious amounts of chemicals. For this reason, numerous research groups are working on developing coating systems and microstructures that prevent water from adhering, hinder ice crystal formation and in turn prevent large surfaces of ice forming.

MICROSTRUCTURED POLYURETHANE COATING

Plasma technologies can be used, for example, to deposit ice-repellent micro- and nanostructured layers of polyurethane and other surfaces. These have a superhydrophobic effect, causing surface water to contract into spherical droplets and roll off. This helps hinder ice formation and reduces ice adhesion by up to 90 %. The anti-icing coating developed at Bremen University of Applied Sciences has already been successfully applied to self-adhesive, impact-resistant polyurethane film. The film can then be applied to the respective object that needs ice protection. Typical applications include aircraft wings, rotor blades, solar panels, overhead power lines, building facades, sports equipment and cooling units.

PYROELECTRIC COATING SYSTEM

At the TU Dresden, researchers are developing active pyroelectric coatings to retard ice formation and minimise ice adhesion to surfaces made of aluminium, steel, glass-fibre reinforced plastic (GRP) and glass. Pyroelectric materials react to temperature fluctuations with a change in charge that in turn influences the bonding conditions for water and ice at the surface layer. Depending on the polarisation of the coating, the effect can be used to reduce or increase ice crystal formation.

Active pyroelectric coatings minimising ice adhesion to the rotor blades of wind turbines
Source: TU Dresden

SALVINIA EFFECT

Some plants and animals such as floating ferns and backswimmers have a highly water-repellent, superhydrophobic skin due to their structured surface. When immersed in water, a stable layer of air forms over their surface. As no water gets between the fine hairs, a layer of air is trapped that has a friction-reducing effect. This phenomenon is described as the Salvinia effect.

In research into the underlying principles of this phenomenon, a group of scientists led by Wilhelm Barthlott at the University of Bonn identified five criteria under which stable air layers can form under water. The Salvinia effect is the product of hydrophobic surfaces which, in combination with nanostructures, result in an extremely superhydrophobic effect. The air is trapped by hair-like microscopic structures of a few micrometres to several millimetres in height that are thinner at their base and are elastic. This elasticity seems to be important to allow the air layer to compress in changing hydrostatic conditions.

As the layer of air between the material surface and the surrounding liquid acts like a lubricating layer, the Salvinia effect could conceivably be utilised for many potential technical applications. For example, when applied to shipbuilding, a friction-reducing coating around a ship hull could lead to a significant reduction in fuel consumption. Friction reductions of up to 30% are expected. Further applications in the field of transport and conduction of water are not yet known.

Scientists at Karlsruhe Institute of Technology (KIT) have presented "NanoFur", a plastic film with a special nanotexture that can effectively separate oil and water after tanker accidents. For its manufacture, a polymer film is placed in a steel mould with microscopic and nanoscopic pores. The mould is heated above the softening temperature of the plastic and the film then pulled from the mould while still warm. This process creates a surface structure like a carpet of nanofibres that mimics the Salvinia effect in nature.

Luminous orange OLED on a graphene electrode
Source: Fraunhofer FEP

GRAPHENE MATERIALS

Graphene is a stable modification of carbon with a two-dimensional structure in which the carbon atoms are arranged in a honeycomb-like pattern. Alongside its exceptional mechanical qualities, most notably its great hardness and extreme tensile strength, graphene is also a particularly good conductor of heat and electrical current, making it ideal for new product developments in the electronics sector, in the field of functional clothing and for printed battery systems. A further recurring area of research concerns possible applications for utilising graphene's transparent properties.

GRAPHENE TEXTILES FOR SMART HEAT TRANSFER

The Italian manufacturer Colmar has developed a textile fabric for winter clothing that exploits graphene's special capacity to conduct heat. The fabric transports heat gene-rated by the athlete to colder areas of the body, promoting optimal blood circulation. In addition, the fabric also reduces the build-up of electrostatic charge.

TRANSPARENT ELECTRONICS

As graphene consists of only a single layer of hexagonally arranged carbon atoms and is thinner than 0.3 nm, it is visually transparent. Research groups around the world have therefore been seeking ways to produce graphene displays and touchscreens. In 2017, the Fraunhofer Institute for Organic Electronics, Electron Beam and Plasma Technol-ogy (FEP) in Dresden succeeded for the first time in producing organic light-emitting diodes (OLEDs) from graphene.

GRAPHENE-BASED FILAMENT PRINTING

Experts predict that many more industries, and the electronics sector in particular, will leverage the potential of additive manufacturing and 3D printing over the next few years. The recent commercial availability of electrically conductive print filaments with graphene will play a significant role.

Foam infiltrated with oil-attracting silanes
Source: Mark Lopez, Argonne National Laboratory

WATER-CLEANSING FILTER MATERIALS

Clean drinking water is a valuable resource all over the world. However, some one billion people worldwide still have poor access to clean drinking water, and in many regions local water supplies are often heavily polluted and contaminated with pathogens and chemicals. The consequences of global warming and the rising global population will further exacerbate this situation in the coming years. To tackle this, numerous new material solutions for filtering systems are being developed to filter pollutants from water and desalinate seawater.

OLEO SPONGE

At the Argonne National Laboratory in Illinois, a research team led by the chemist Jeffrey Elam has developed a sponge based on regular polyurethane foam that can recover oil from seawater better than conventional solutions using woven mats of wool and human hair. The foam was modified by infiltrating it with oil-attracting silanes so that the sponge has a greater chemical affinity for oils and kerosene.

Water filter made of anti-bacterial cellulose fibres
Source: KTH Royal Institute of Technology

Functionality of a graphene filter
Source: University of Manchester

POLYELECTROLYTE-MODIFIED CELLULOSE FIBRES

Scientists at KTH Royal Institute of Technology in Stockholm are working on a water filter made of antibacterial cellulose fibres derived from various tree species. To purify the water, the filter is soaked in a positively charged polymer. Bacteria and viruses with a negative charge are attracted and filtered from the water. In contrast to the sand filter or textile filter systems commonly used, this method avoids poisons or toxins leaching into the water. After use, the cellulose filter can simply be burnt. The filter is also suitable for use in regions with little infrastructure as it does not require electricity. The researchers see further fields of use in medical technology, such as for sanitary towels and bandages, and in the packaging industry.

GRAPHENE FILTER FOR DRINKING WATER FROM THE SEA

Existing technologies for desalination and the treatment of seawater are costly and energy-intensive. In 2017, scientists from Manchester developed a graphene sieve that could greatly simplify seawater desalination. Graphene has a hexagonal honey-comb-like structure of carbon atoms and is only one atom thick. For the filter, the British researchers used the chemical derivative graphene oxide. When dissolved in an ink and applied to a porous surface, graphene oxide produces a membrane with openings smaller than one nanometre. While water molecules can pass through it, salts are reliably filtered out.

Textile with magnetically
active fibres

Source: Professor Markus Holzbach,
Institut für Materialsdesign (IMD),
HfG Offenbach/Main, in cooperation
with BMW AG

MAGNETIC AND MAGNETORHEOLOGICAL MATERIALS

Magnetic qualities play an important role in the controlling of surfaces and implementation of shape-changing qualities. Various development projects are underway
that attempt to endow materials with magnetic or magnetorheological properties that
they would not normally have. Magnetorheological substances are typically fluids that
respond to the activation of an electric or magnetic field by becoming more viscous,
even to the point of becoming a solid.

MAGNETIC FABRICS

A series of projects undertaken at the Institute for Material Design (IMD) at the Hochschule für Gestaltung (HfG) Offenbach/Main examined the development of new functional surfaces for interaction in mobility solutions. Alongside experimental material samples, physical and digital models and mock-ups were developed for various
application scenarios. In the project "Magnetic Fabrics", Lilian Dedio shows how incorporating magnetic fibres into a textile makes it possible to create a surface with a
controllable arrangement.

Magnetic wood block
Source: ETH Zurich, Vivian Merk

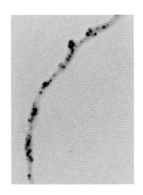

Magnetic cellulose
Source: Cellutech

MAGNETIC WOOD

Vivian Merk, a scientist at the ETH Zurich, has developed a process that makes it possible to magnetise wood by embedding iron oxide particles deeply within the cell structure. The wood is first softened in an acid solution containing ferric chloride salts. The piece of wood is then removed, and a precipitation reaction is triggered in a strong leach solution. Black nanoparticles of iron oxide flocculate and settle in the inner cell walls of the wood structure. Potential applications are under development, in particular in the automotive industry.

MAGNETIC CELLULOSE

The composite material consists of nanocellulose and magnetic nanoparticles. Using a special process, the magnetic nanoparticles are evenly distributed on the cellulose nanofibrils, giving the material not only good mechanical properties but also magnetic properties. Potential application areas include electrical devices, imaging systems and medical diagnostics. Scientists have already succeeded in producing ultra-thin loudspeakers using magnetic nanocellulose with a thickness of just 50 μm.

A magnetorheological elastomer changes density under
the influence of a magnetic
field
Source: Fraunhofer ISC

MAGNETORHEOLOGICAL ELASTOMERS

Elastomers are soft polymers with high extensibility and are widely used in numerous technical applications, for example for seals or as vibration-damping bearings. One of the key properties of elastomers is their hardness, which can be adapted to meet the needs of a specific application. The ability to selectively modify the hardness of an elastomer surface makes it possible to change how it feels. Such behaviour can be achieved using magnetorheological elastomers.

Electroluminescent display
with a rivulet of water
Source: Luke Franzke, Zürcher
Hochschule der Künste ZHdK

PHONO-LUMINOUS PAPER AND LIQUID LIGHT

Phono-luminous paper emits light signals that respond to touch. At the same time, the material can be made to vibrate, emitting sounds. The material was developed as part of a series of experimental research projects by Luke Franzke at Zurich University of the Arts (ZHdK) focusing on the utility of ephemeral materials.

Unlike any other audio-visual touch display, phono-luminous paper is completely analogue. The unique combination of different components enables the paper to act as a sensor, a display and a sound generator. The interactive capabilities are programmed during material fabrication, but the computation happens inside the material itself.

Light emissions on phono-
luminous paper
Source: Luke Franzke, Zürcher
Hochschule der Künste ZHdK

Phono-luminous paper is produced by screen-printing various electrically active layers onto the paper's surface, which is then given a protective layer of polyester film. The fabrication process is cost-effective and can scale to mass-production. Very little power is required to achieve the effect, making it possible to produce in large sizes such as the size of an entire wall.

The phenomena of light and sound are produced by the combination of electroluminescence and electroacoustic transduction, both driven by an AC power supply. The material, together with the induction coils in the AC power supply, forms a resonant circuit, which responds to the application of pressure on the material. The material can generate tones at frequencies between 340 and 810 Hz, while the light ranges from cool green to blue colour temperatures. Additional colours are also possible using additives during the fabrication process.

In a further project, Luke Franzke also developed an electroluminescent display under the name of "Liquid Light", where water on the surface is used for the function of the display. A particular light is emitted as the droplets run off the surface.

Light-emitting plants
Source: MIT; photo: Seon-Yeong Kwak

LUMINOUS PLANTS

Light-emitting plants such as those seen in the blockbuster film Avatar are no longer science fiction according to recent publications by a group of researchers from MIT in the USA. The scientists led by chemistry professor Michael Strano have succeeded in infusing living watercress with luminous nanoparticles, causing them to glow for a few hours.

The light spectrum of the particles is similar to that of glow-worms in the yellow-green range. Although the luminosity was just a faint glow lasting up to four hours, the researchers expect in future to be able to use nanotechnology to give plants special properties. They also plan to make larger plants such as a ficus shrub or yucca palm glow.

To achieve this, fluorescent nanoparticles known as luciferins were introduced into the plants' biomass. This is the same substance that gives glow-worms their glow. The luciferins were transported together with special polymers using silicon nanoglobules as a carrier and absorbed into the plant via microscopically small leaf pores in the leaves. These stomata help the plant regulate its moisture content and close if the plant is in danger of losing too much vital moisture.

The scientists at MIT envisage being able to illuminate entire streets using luminous trees. According to Strano's calculations, it would be possible to use the principle to achieve the luminous intensity required for street lighting.

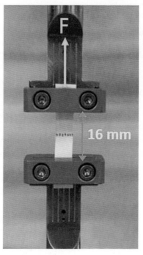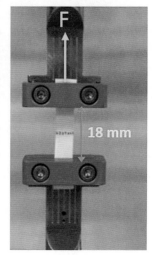

10 mm

16 mm

18 mm

20 n

Self-healing polymer ma-
terial for flexible electronic
applications
Source: Pennsylvania State University

SELF-HEALING MATERIALS

Materials with self-healing properties are the dream of many architects and product developers as they have the potential to extend the life of a product, a coating or a road surface enormously. Until recently, research had concentrated on self-healing solutions in which scratches in paintwork or cracks in asphalt could self-repair. In the last few years, focus has shifted to concepts in which materials that have been separated can be reconnected.

SELF-HEALING POLYUREA-URETHANE (PUU)

A self-healing elastomer based on urea and carbamates was developed at the Cidetec Institute in San Sebastian, Spain. When the material is sliced and the cut surfaces are placed face-to-face, it takes about two hours for the material to re-join. The process is based on a metathesis reaction of aromatic disulfides, takes place at room temperature and has an efficiency of 97 %. After the process, the cut material parts are firmly reconnected and can withstand great forces.

SELF-HEALING MATERIALS FOR ELECTRONIC APPLICATIONS

Another spectacular project was developed at Penn State University for flexible electronic systems in garments. These so-called wearables frequently have to withstand strong mechanical deformation and are bent or compressed, requiring new solutions for the materials used. To address this problem, US scientists led by Qing Wang have developed a self-healing material that, once healed, also restores all the properties required for electronic applications. Alongside mechanical strength, these include thermal and electrical conductivity as well as breakdown strength to protect against surges and dielectric or insulating qualities. The healing process is based on boron nitride nanosheets incorporated into a polymer that join together at their surfaces via functionalised hydrogen bonding groups.

SELF-HEALING THERMOPLASTIC POLYURETHANE (TPU)

Under the name "Estane VSN 9000", the company Lubrizol has developed a TPU for the specific requirements of design parts subject to high loads. The material is lightweight and has a strong elastic memory after bending and is therefore particularly suitable for applications such as spectacle frames. Its standout feature is its self-healing capability: scratches disappear after a bath in hot water at a temperature of about 90 °C.

8

RENEWABLE ENERGY AND ENERGY PRODUCTION

Moss cells that generate energy
Source: Fabienne Felder

In many large cities, small, periodically blinking boxes have begun to appear on street signs, traffic lights, in public transport, on lanterns or facades. These sensors collect vast quantities of data from their surroundings and constitute a fundamental building block for the smart city of the future. They measure temperature, humidity, noise levels, signals from communication devices and light levels, and relay any relevant changes to a smart system. Intelligent sensor technologies will become increasingly widespread in Europe as smart systems for regulating traffic, intelligent parking, adaptive lighting, signalling systems and waste management are put into practice. Throughout Europe, vast sums have been invested in smart city concepts and research into artificial intelligence and industry observers predict that new business segments will emerge over the next seven years with a market volume totalling some 1.6 trillion euros.

With increasing digitisation and the accompanying widespread adoption of networked devices as part of the Internet of Things, it is becoming increasingly vital that these small data collectors function reliably. They need to be able to transmit data independently, be maintenance-free and also energy self-sufficient, as the devices are often difficult to reach and cannot always be connected to a power supply. For this reason, applications such as those monitoring agricultural land for efficient water use or seamlessly tracking goods have until now been problematic.

Successful advances in semiconductor technology have heralded the advent of integrated circuits with extremely low power consumption that can be supplied by so-called energy harvesters that capture energy from the immediate environment. The energy sources are as diverse as they are abundant and illustrate the wealth of such untapped sources available on the planet. Alongside sunlight, heat and wind, further renewable energy sources include vibrations from machines, temperature differences in pipelines and even biochemical processes in living organisms such as plants, animals and bacteria. Humans themselves, as active organisms, are likewise a potential source of energy. Energy converters incorporated into textiles or shoe soles will soon be available that provide sufficient energy to power wearables such as fitness trackers, digital glasses or smartwatches. Energy harvesters look set to be a promising technological building block for the development of future smart cities.

It is envisaged that by 2050 Europe's electrical power will be supplied entirely by renewable energy sources such as solar power, wind energy and biomass. According to experts from the LUT University of Technology in Finland and the Energy Watch Group, this goal is both realistic and economically competitive compared with today's conventional fossil fuel and nuclear energy-based systems. However, power generation from sun, wind and water is subject to natural fluctuations, which is problematic for industrialised nations with varying climates such as Germany. To ensure a constant supply of energy across Europe, scientists and engineers are working on new energy storage and battery systems. Electricity can also be stored in pumped-storage plants and converted into hydrogen for distribution on demand via an intelligent networked system.

A further factor that will contribute to the successful transition to renewable energy sources will be technological advances in key components of these systems. Making solar cells more efficient, thermogenerators more cost-effective or batteries without heavy metals will provide politicians with ever stronger arguments to push forward changes to energy policies. In January 2019, for example, a commission recommended the phasing out of Germany's coal-fired power stations.

Current Window
Source: Marjan van Aubel

TRANSPARENT AND ORGANIC PHOTOVOLTAICS

Organic photovoltaics (OPV) looks set to be the next major innovation in the field of solar energy generation. The ability to print solar-active dyes onto foils that are flexible and transparent marks a big step forward – one which will open up numerous new design possibilities, especially for architecture. Until now, their low energy yield compared to silicon-based PV modules has limited the market uptake of OPV-based solutions, but recent successful developments may soon change the market dramatically.

SOLAR CONCRETE WALL

Europe's first solar concrete wall in Herne, Germany, by the pioneering tech-company Heliatek makes a convincing case for the profitability of integral organic PV systems. Facing south-west with an installed capacity of 1 kWp, the concrete wall delivers around 500 kWh of energy per year. Given the 130 million m² of concrete surfaces erected every year, this concept could have enormous potential. Integrating organic photovoltaics into building surfaces can contribute significantly to a building's power supply and significantly improve the CO_2 balance of office buildings and warehouses, especially in large cities. Designers and architects have a wide range of design options at their disposal with regard to colour schemes and layout of the foils.

CURRENT TABLE

To make use of solar energy in building interiors, the designers at Caventou in London have begun incorporating photovoltaics into everyday objects. Their first product is the Current Table, a desk with a glass top with dye-sensitised solar cells on its underside. Marjan van Aubel and her colleagues have previously applied dye-sensitised solar cells to a window to create an electricity-generating 'stained' glass window. A USB port for charging a mobile phone or camera is built into the window sill. A further notable advantage of OPV technology is that energy can also be generated from artificial light.

SOLAR GLASS BLOCKS

In Palermo, Sicily, scientists led by Rossella Corrao have developed 3D glass components with integral OPV dye-sensitised solar cells. The solar glass blocks are marketed under the name "Smart Building Skin" and can be assembled into multifunctional panels to help reduce the overall energy consumption of buildings. The solar modules are environmentally friendly and fully recyclable and can be produced in different colours, shapes and degrees of transparency to meet different design needs. For easy installation, a mounting system has been developed that also anchors the solar modules to the load-bearing structure.

Current Table
Source: Marjan van Aubel;
photo: Mitch Payne

Europe's first solar concrete
wall
Source: Heliatek, Reckli

Solar glass modules with
integrated dye-sensitised
solar cells
Source: sbskin

Transparent solar panel
Source: Michigan State University;
photo: Yimu Zhao

TRANSPARENT SOLAR PANEL

Researchers at Michigan State University (MSU) have developed a solar concentrator that can be placed on a window pane, generates electricity and is invisible to the human eye. With an efficiency of 1%, the American scientists currently see most potential for use in mobile electronics as part of tablet and mobile phone displays. The goal of the next development phase is to improve efficiency to 5% so that it can compete with existing semi-transparent cells, which have an efficiency of 7%.

Fragments of broken solar cells
Source: Ryszard Dzikowski

MINI SOLAR CELLS

Crystalline solar cells are used in around 90 % of global solar module production. Of these, some 10 % are discarded due to defects or breakage. Only sufficiently large fragments are laser-cut into smaller cells for making small modules. The rest is melted down as a waste product and processed into polysilicon.

MINI SOLAR CELLS FROM BROKEN SOLAR-CELL FRAGMENTS

In Berlin, Ryszard Dzikowski has developed a technology for producing mini solar cells from fragments of solar cells using simple tools. The inventor calculates that one kilogram of solar fragments can be used to produce between 1,600 and 1,800 mini solar cells measuring 20 × 20 mm, a quantity sufficient to make 130 to 150 solar lamps at a price of under 10 USD each. Such lamps could replace expensive kerosene lamps in developing countries. The solar cells are simple enough for non-experts to use and assemble themselves. Mini solar cells could be used for a variety of purposes ranging from solar battery chargers, locating systems and solar lights to active RFID systems and radio tags for animal livestock or transponder systems.

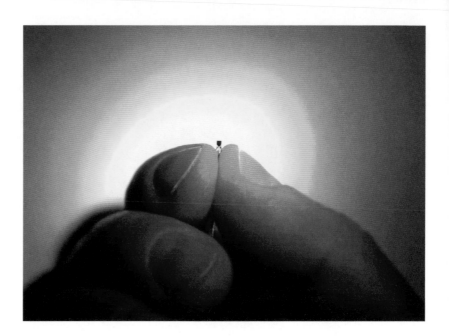

Mini solar cells
Source: Ryszard Dzikowski

MINI SOLAR CELLS FOR GARMENTS

Mini solar cells also offer increasing potential for use in smart wearables. Scientists at Nottingham Trent University in Great Britain have developed solar cells that are 3 mm long and 1.5 mm wide and can be incorporated into textiles for sustainably generating energy. For example, a wearable could supply a fitness tracker with electricity. According to the researchers, an item of clothing would need some 2,000 mini solar cells to charge a smartphone. The mini solar cells are almost invisible to the human eye and their small size means that they have little impact on the wearing comfort of a garment. The team has already presented a prototype of its concept with an area of 5 × 5 cm that contains 200 miniature solar cells.

Cylindrical liquid lens for
concentrated photovoltaics
Source: Ryszard Dzikowski

LIQUID LENSES

Liquid lenses are used to concentrate rays of light in order to significantly increase the efficiency of photovoltaic modules. Due to the very high concentration factor of concentrated light, liquid lenses can help reduce the required surface area of photovoltaic panels to a fraction of existing systems and with them the size of solar thermal power plants. In recent years, a number of interesting approaches for utilising liquid lenses have been presented.

CYLINDRICAL LIQUID LENS

An innovative form of cylindrical lenses with the properties of several spherical lenses was presented by Lumicell in Berlin. The water-filled liquid lens consists of a transparent, hollow volume made of plastic or glass that is convex or biconvex on one side. This assembly can concentrate light by a factor of up to 2,000 times. As the materials are very inexpensive, the cylindrical lens can be manufactured in any conceivable size and shape. Its composition and function have given rise to new, innovative optical solutions that are suitable for use in both concentrated photovoltaics (CPV) and concentrated solar thermal power plants (CSP).

Spherical concentrator
Source: André Brössel, Rawlemon

SPHERICAL CONCENTRATOR

The architect André Brössel presented a glass ball filled with liquid that acts as a solar collector concentrating light rays on a focal point for use with photovoltaic cells or heat-driven mini-generators. Tests in Barcelona have shown that spherical lenses greatly increase light output. Compared to conventional concentrating systems, spherical lenses are expected to double yields. The solar collector has the advantage of working not just on sunny days, but also when the sky is overcast or even at night: the glass ball can concentrate lunar rays and convert them into electrical energy. Spherical lenses are much more efficient in diffuse light conditions than Fresnel lenses, and are also not dependent on the direction of light, thanks to a specially developed swivel mechanism. At present, however, they are still costly to manufacture.

Rawlemon has brought the concept onto the market under the name "beta.ray" in the form of a solar collector comprised of a large number of solid plastic spheres. It can provide twice the amount of energy as a conventional solar panel and can, for example, be installed into building facades. Using a dual-axis tracking system, the collector aligns the spheres at an optimum angle to the light source. A small-scale version for recharging mobile phones has already been marketed and a large-scale solution for glass facades in office buildings is currently being developed.

Plant-e in function test
Source: Plant-e

BIOCHEMICAL ENERGY PRODUCTION

Functional principle of the Plant-e energy-generation process
Source: Plant-e

Plant-based microbial fuel cells generate electricity from living plants and, in combination with efficient urban agriculture, represent a potentially promising technological means of producing sustainable power from renewable sources. Bacteria in the soil digest organic compounds exuded by plant roots following photosynthesis, giving off electrons that are captured by an electrode and converted into electricity.

PLANT-E

Plant-e, a spin-off company founded at the University of Wageningen in Holland, has developed a technology for generating electrical energy from living plants that will in future make it possible for green roofs to supply energy. According to the developers' projections, the system will be able to generate a potential output of $0.5\,MW/km^2$.

Plants produce oxygen and organic substances such as glucose ($C_6H_{12}O_6$) through photosynthesis. Glucose is transported to the roots of the plant, where it is digested by bacteria, in the process giving off free electrons and protons. The potential gradient of electrical charge necessary to cause a current to flow is established using a system comprising an anode, a cathode and a membrane that separates the soil from water. The carbon electrodes are inert and do not react with their surroundings. According to the company, a $15\,m^2$ Plant-e system on a green roof can power a smartphone. A prototype of the system in the company's home town of Wageningen is already powering LED street lighting.

Moss FM radio
Source: Fabienne Felder

Alternatively ten moss cells
can be used to power a
digital clock
Source: Fabienne Felder

MOSS FM RADIO

In collaboration with scientists from the University of Cambridge in the UK, Fabienne Felder developed the world's first moss radio powered by photo microbial fuel cells (Photo-MFCs). To ensure a constant supply of energy, Fabienne Felder uses the output of photosynthesis during the day and the naturally occurring bacterial processes of plant respiration at night. Additional bacterial processes in the Photo-MFCs enable the cells to produce electricity in the dark. To generate power, an array of ten moss cells are used, equipped with a composite of water-storing, conductive and vegetable materials. To ensure a constant stable power supply, the moss cells charge a battery that powers the radio. For continuous operation, all moss cells must always be kept moist and placed in a sunny location. This is the first time an electrical device has been supplied solely by the use of plants.

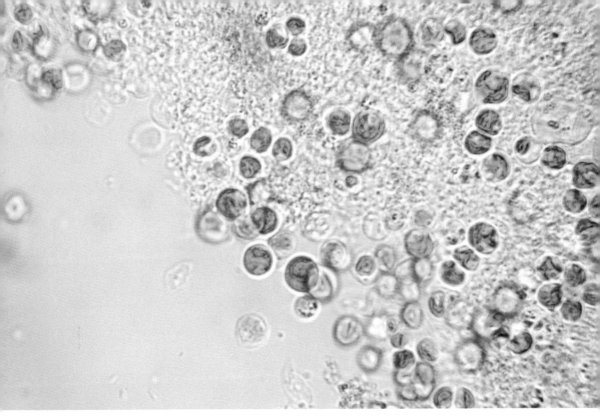

Chlorella vulgaris algae under the microscope. Algae have great potential in the fields of bio-energy and health
Source: Fabienne Felder

Algae thermometer
Source: Fabienne Felder

ALGAE-OPERATED THERMOMETER

Fabienne Felder's exploration of photo-microbial fuel cells continued at Rhode Island School of Design, where she developed the world's first household electrical appliance driven by Photo-MFCs in the form of a thermometer. Microalgae are used to power a commercially available temperature sensor and LCD. It ran continuously for several months as part of the exhibition "Biodesign: from Inspiration to Integration" in the USA and was the only living exhibit.

Experimental set-up for harvesting energy from a crab
Photo: Haute Innovation

ENERGY FROM ANIMAL ORGANISMS

Alongside plants, animal organisms can also be harnessed to produce energy, albeit in minute quantities. Research projects at three universities, the Clarkson in New York, Case Western Reserve in Cleveland and the Université Joseph Fourier in Grenoble, have discovered a means of converting glucose and other compounds from living organisms into electrical energy using enzymes in biological fuel cells. This capacity exists for as long as the organism lives. A potential future application could, for example, be a muscle-operated heart pacemaker.

The following experiments were carried out at the various universities:

LOBSTER (POWER OUTPUT: 12 MICROWATTS)

The scientists implanted an enzyme-coated film of carbon nanotubes as electrodes onto the back of the crustacean. These biofuel cells generated a voltage amounting to about one-third that of an AAA battery.

COCKROACH (POWER OUTPUT: UNSPECIFIED)

The researchers used capacitors to store electrical power from a cockroach and used the energy to transmit radio signals. The researchers' vision was to develop a cyborg insect that could be controlled by a joystick.

SNAIL (POWER OUTPUT: 7.45 MICROWATT)

When a snail is allowed to feed on carrots, it produces a sufficiently large quantity of body fluids to power a pacemaker. The underlying organic mechanism could be put to use in humans to power implantable devices using energy from a patient's body.

CLAM (POWER OUTPUT: 37 MICROWATT)

In their investigations of the electrical potential of clams, the scientists found that an array of three clams purchased at a normal grocery store was sufficient to generate enough power for a tiny electric motor. A break was necessary between each of the test series to allow the clams to replenish their blood sugar levels.

RAT (POWER OUTPUT: 6.5 MICROWATT)

After implanting electrodes in the abdomen of a 500g rat, the researchers were able to draw an electric current from the blood of the rat for three months. In future, the scientists envisage being able to produce artificial organs powered by their host.

Swing Harvester for generating electrical energy from the swinging motion of a leg when running
Source: Klevis Ylli, Hahn-Schickard-Gesellschaft

KINETIC ENERGY CONVERTERS

Nowadays a smartphone or smartwatch is all one needs to count steps, monitor one's fitness or track one's radius of activity. Today's affluent societies are trying to counteract health risks such as diabetes and cardiovascular diseases arising from poor nutrition and insufficient exercise. New technical developments are also surfacing: for example, fitness equipment and sports shoes that make it possible to generate energy from human movement, contributing a further alternative means of energy generation.

VOLTAGE CONVERTERS FOR ENERGY-GENERATING FITNESS

René Eick was one of the first to recognise the possibilities of generating energy in the fitness sector. In his GreenGym fitness club in the Prenzlauer Berg district of Berlin, he equipped a total of 18 bicycles and steppers with voltage converters that utilise the athletes' kinetic energy to power the studio. Fitness enthusiasts produce on average 80 W as they put their effort into pedalling the bicycle ergometer, enough to recharge a smartphone several times over. Sockets attached to the training equipment can be used to charge device batteries.

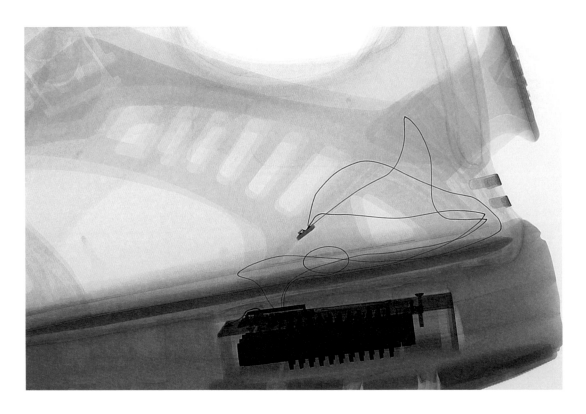

Shock Harvester incorporated
into a running shoe
Source: Klevis Ylli,
Hahn-Schickard-Gesellschaft

SHOCK AND SWING HARVESTERS

Developers at the Hahn-Schickard-Gesellschaft in Freiburg are pursuing a similar idea by incorporating electronics into a running shoe that transform the impact forces (shock harvester) and kinetic energy of the moving leg (swing harvester) into electrical energy and store it in a battery. Both concepts employ the physical principle of induction: electrical energy is generated by movement of a magnetic field along a coil. Such shoes will in future make it possible to power devices that measure one's pulse or step frequency without first having to charge a rechargeable battery.

PIEZOELECTRIC ENERGY SYSTEMS

Inexpensive plastics with piezoelectric properties have been successfully trialled in textiles as a means of generating electricity. When woven as yarn into the fabric, the movement of the wearer causes the material to stretch or compress, thereby producing electrical impulses. Jackets with integral piezo fibres utilize the wearer's movements, or even the impact of raindrops, to generate sufficient energy to charge portable devices such as mobile telephones or to cause the jacket to glow in the dark.

GARMENTS WITH PIEZO FIBRES

Scientists at Chalmers University of Technology in Gothenburg have successfully developed current-generating textiles using piezo technology. The Swedes use a piezoelectric thread which they weave together with electrically conductive yarn into a stretchable textile. Each individual piezo fibre consists of 24 electrically conductive fibres encased in a piezoelectric sheath. Stretching the fabric generates sufficient energy to let an LED glow or supply power to small devices such as a calculator or a digital watch. This effect can be enhanced by using moisture: when wet, the fibres are coated with water, thus increasing the conductivity of all the components.

TWISTRON

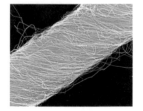

Twisted yarn with piezo-
electric properties
Source: University of Dallas

Researchers at the University of Dallas have developed "Twistron", yarn that produces an electrical charge when stretched. The twisted yarn is woven from carbon nanotubes which, in combination with electrolytes, exhibit piezoelectric properties and can generate electricity. This particular combination occurs when garments are worn on the skin, as human sweat also contains electrolytes. When woven into a fabric, the yarn can harvest electrical energy from the wearer's movements, making batteries for mobile devices potentially superfluous. The fabric is so sensitive that even a person's breathing creates sufficient movement to supply sensors with energy. This capacity could be used, for example, to monitor a patient's breathing. The researchers use a solid polymer containing salts to coat the threads. The twisted yarn can also be used to generate energy from wave movements in the sea: initial tests of yarn attached to a weight on the ocean floor and a floater have demonstrated that the torsion and elongation of the yarn produced by passing waves can be used to generate energy.

Detail of the power producing
BH03 concept tyre
Source: GoodYear

PIEZOELECTRIC MATERIALS FOR
ENERGY-PRODUCING TYRES

At the International Motor Show in Geneva in 2015, the GoodYear tyre specialists presented a concept for a tyre that can generate electricity from heat and deformation. The tyre employs both thermoelectric and piezoelectric materials to recover as much energy as possible from vehicle motion. The thermoelectric material converts into electrical energy the heat accumulated by the tyre through friction when rolling, or absorbed from the sun and surroundings by the tyre's black texture when motionless. At the same time, so-called piezo actuators convert structural deformations in the tyre caused by mechanical impact into electrical energy. The various materials are incorporated into a 3D mesh that forms the inner, supporting structure of the tyre. Around the three-dimensional structural layer is a channel to reduce hydroplaning and an outer sound-absorbing tread.

Application scenario for an
underground station
Source: Charlotte Slingsby

Moya Power in detail
Source: Charlotte Slingsby

MOYA POWER

Under the name of "Moya Power", Charlotte Slingsby from South Africa has developed a technology at the Royal College of Art in London for converting kinetic energy from air movement into electrical energy using a transparent textile sheet with long plastic strands. The micro power plant is made of the fluoroplastic PVDF, which, after appropriate polarisation, exhibits a stronger piezoelectric effect than many other polymers. When the material is set in motion, it absorbs mechanical energy and converts the movement into electrical impulses that can be fed into the electric circuit. The designer estimates that one square metre of her electricity-generating textile generates about 10 % of the energy generated by conventional photovoltaic panels. It is intended to complement existing technologies such as solar or wind power plants and can be used in tunnels, under motorway bridges, in underground shafts or other air corridors as well as rivers. An initial pilot test is planned for the Elisabeth Line of the London Underground network.

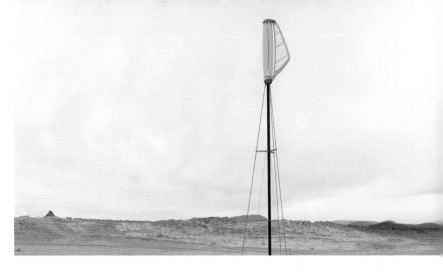

Wind power plant with
inverse kinematics
Source: Ferdinand Drechsel

SMALL WIND TURBINES FOR URBAN AREAS

Wind energy now plays an increasingly important role in the power supply mix, accounting in 2017 for 16.1 % of gross electricity generation in Germany. In addition to the construction of large-scale plants and offshore wind farms, developers are also working on small wind turbines to supply energy to businesses and private homes in urban areas. The ideas range from small wind turbines for facades to modular systems or spherical systems independent of the wind direction.

WIND POWER PLANT USING INVERSE KINEMATICS

So-called wind concentrators with a horizontal axis of rotation or small wind turbines with a vertical rotor (e. g. a Savonius or Darrieus rotor) are already available on the market. "Invento" is an alternative wind power plant based on the principle of inverse kinematics and was developed at Darmstadt University of Applied Sciences at the department headed by Tom Philipps. It transforms wind energy into electrical energy by turning it into a rotary motion that corresponds to the principle of inverse kinematics. The angle of the rotor blades in relation to wind direction is essential for efficiency. The turbine is a slow rotor, which, in contrast to high-speed rotors, can turn at low wind speeds, making the system particularly suitable for small wind power plants. Low-speed turbines are driven purely by the thrust of the wind and their speed of rotation is always lower or at best equal to the wind speed. Such systems can respond to lower wind speeds, since the force vector points exactly in the direction of rotation when the air mass meets the rotor. At high wind speeds, the mechanical load on an inverse kinematic rotor is significantly greater than on a high-speed rotor, making such systems ideal where limited space is available.

Modular wind power plant
Source: MOWEA, Berlin

MODULAR WIND POWER PLANT

Mowea, a start-up from Berlin, has brought out the world's first modular wind turbine designed for the practicable and economical supply of private wind energy. The system consists of a large number of small, highly efficient wind generators that can be connected to form differently dimensioned systems according to energy requirements. Its key advantage lies in its scalability using cost-effective, standardised components. The wind turbine system can cover power requirements ranging from 400 W up to medium kW levels. The modular approach means the system can also be used in densely built-up areas, for example for family houses, on mobile phone masts or on low-rise industrial buildings.

O-Wind turbine for frequently
changing wind directions
Source: Nicolas Orellana, Yaseen
Noorani

O-WIND TURBINE

Students at the University of Lancaster have developed a spherical turbine for locations with frequently changing wind directions. In urban areas in particular, wind often swirls around buildings of different heights, and small changes in wind speed can lead to spontaneous changes in wind direction. Nicolas Orellana and Yaseen Noorani make use of Bernoulli's principle for their development: in the 18th century, the Swiss mathematician investigated flowing liquids and found that pressure always decreases for higher flow velocities. Building on this, the young engineers opted for a spherical design for their O-Wind turbine, which is only 25 cm in size. They arranged gill-like openings vertically and horizontally around a single axis of rotation that narrow inwards. Its round shape means the wind has to travel a longer distance around the outside of the turbine than inside the turbine. The resulting pressure difference produces a mechanical axial rotation that is converted into electricity.

Microturbine for harvesting
energy from water flows in
drainpipes
Source: Blue Freedom

ENERGY-HARVESTING
PIPELINES

Energy-autonomous
flow-rate monitoring system
that can be read remotely
Source: Fraunhofer IIS, Heiko
Wörrlein

Energy-harvesting technology makes it possible to generate small quantities of electrical energy from the environment in order to power electronic systems such as sensors, radio transmitters or displays without needing an external electricity supply. Various scientists and companies have discovered a promising source of energy in the flow of liquids in pipelines.

OVAL GEAR METERS

Scientists at the Fraunhofer Institute for Integrated Circuits (IIS) have succeeded in generating energy from volume flows in downpipes, sewage systems and pipelines using a custom-developed oval gear meter. The technology provides a maintenance-free way to remotely read data from pipelines and fuel pumps to determine the amount of fuel that has passed. Previously, an electric power supply or batteries were needed to measure and transmit the recorded data. In many cases, the cost of providing an electricity supply to the flow meter was prohibitive, making remote reading an uneconomical proposition.

Through a suitable arrangement of magnets and permanently installed coils, the rotary movement of the oval gear meter can generate around 20 mW at a flow rate of 50 l/min, which is sufficient to power a radio transmitter module without the need for additional batteries. The recorded data can then be transmitted wirelessly. The ability to remotely read meters makes it possible to monitor and measure flow rates for a range of applications and is in many countries mandatory for pipelines and fuel pumps.

Small hydroelectric power
plant for flowing water
Source: Blue Freedom

MICROTURBINES IN DRAINPIPES

The developers at Blue Freedom in Bavaria have gone a step further and produced a microturbine for drainage pipes. A total of four trillion litres of water pass through drains around the world every year. The microturbine makes it possible to generate electricity from even small water movements. The system is suitable for use with tap water and sewage pipes as well as pipes in sewage treatment plants.

SMALL-SCALE HYDROELECTRIC POWER PLANT FOR FLOWING WATER

The microturbine builds on the company's experience of building the world's smallest and lightest hydroelectric power plant. With a diameter of 20 cm, it weighs just 400 g. The microturbine makes it possible to generate electricity for small electrical devices such as smartphones, digicams and lamps from a flow velocity of 0.5 m/s or more. Blue Freedom has a capacity of more than 5,000 mAh with an output of at least 5 W. To increase its capacity, additional energy banks can be connected to two USB ports.

Paper battery with an output
of between 0.1 and 100 mW
Source: Fuelium

ENERGY STORAGE DEVICES WITHOUT HEAVY METALS

The use of disposable batteries results in around 40,000 t of hazardous waste every year in Germany alone. As batteries contain heavy metals, they must be disposed of appropriately. For household use, battery systems that do not contain toxic substances and can be disposed of as part of normal household waste would be highly desirable.

PAPER BATTERY

The Spanish company Fuelium has developed a paper battery that, unlike conventional lithium batteries, does not contain any toxic substances or heavy metals. Instead, the energy store makes use of an electrochemical reaction. A liquid test medium is transported to a sensor by the capillary effect of the paper. According to the scientists, the voltage can be adjusted between one and six volts at a power output of 0.1 to 100 mW. The developers envisage the battery being used to power electrical devices with low power requirements, for example in the medical field for powering in vitro diagnostic devices for testing blood sugar levels or the hormonal balance of patients. Currently, such disposable measuring devices are powered by lithium button batteries, which then often end up in household waste, even when only 1% of the battery charge has been used. Fuelium batteries can be tailored precisely to the respective application, and their low production costs mean that they can also benefit hospitals in developing countries.

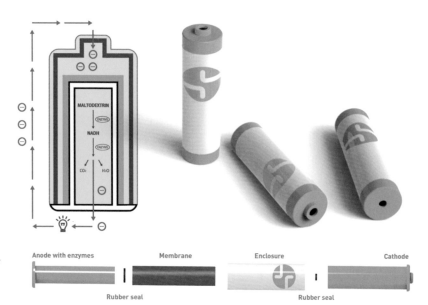

Functionality and structure of the sugar battery
Source: Dennis Rittel, Ana Maria Garcia and Soichiro Katayama

Anode with enzymes   Membrane   Enclosure   Cathode

Rubber seal   Rubber seal

SUGAR BATTERY

A group of researchers led by Y.H. Percival Zhang presented a system for a sugar battery that can store 15 times more energy than comparable lithium-ion-based technologies. The idea was taken up by the industrial design students Dennis Rittel, Ana Maria Garcia and Soichiro Katayama from Darmstadt University of Applied Sciences and translated into a commercially available format. The designers' intention is that sugar-based fuel cells will in future be used to power MP3 players, remote controls and other electronic devices. The system employs maltrodextrin, a sugar usually used in sports, dissolved in water. Through the addition of enzymes, the sugar degrades in a biochemical process into water and carbon dioxide, in the process releasing a large amount of energy. This energy, which athletes convert into physical activity, must be stored temporarily for use in electrical product scenarios. To this end, the designers developed a battery housing made of polylactide (PLA) along with a special charging station. Once the sugar has degraded, the battery is placed in the charger, where the remaining liquid is sucked out of the housing under vacuum and replenished with fresh sugar solution. Special rubber membranes at the top and bottom of the battery serve as discharge and recharge ports.

The functional principle of
Gravity Storage
Source: Professor Eduard Heindl

GRAVITY STORAGE

One of the greatest challenges in using wind and solar energy is the need to balance out diurnal and seasonal fluctuations. After all, photovoltaic systems cannot generate electricity at night. To maintain a constant supply of energy in a grid system powered predominantly by renewable energy sources, substantially larger storage capabilities are required than are currently available in order to cover prolonged periods of low wind or little sunshine.

Eduard Heindl from Stuttgart has developed a concept for an intermediate storage facility that can supply an entire locality with energy over a longer period of time. His Gravity Storage concept is based on the idea of lifting a huge mass of rock – a mobile piston of rock below ground that has been cut free of its surrounding rock – by pumping water under pressure beneath it to raise it, storing the energy used as gravitational potential for later use. When the regular energy supply ebbs, the water under pressure beneath the rock is discharged and fed through a turbine, where it is converted into electrical energy using a generator, much like in conventional hydroelectric plants. The capacity of the system to store energy depends on the size of the rock piston. To be competitive, a gravity storage tank should have a diameter of at least 100 m. According to the developer's calculations, a piston diameter of 250 m results in costs of 200 USD/kWh capacity.

The storage facility can be constructed employing methods already used in conventional mining and tunnelling. The storage system requires two main seals: the surfaces of the cylindrical chamber and of the piston itself, and a sealing ring around the piston. The piston and the surrounding cylinder of the water chamber are sealed with a geomembrane to prevent water seeping into the surrounding rock. To seal the gap between the rock piston and the surrounding cylinder, a ring-shaped seal is used that rolls against a metal surface. The operating principle involves slowly raising and lowering the huge rock piston. At present, the concept exists only as a prototype.

MULTIFERROIC MATERIALS FOR ENDLESS BATTERIES

The purple double line represents the additional iron oxide layer that makes the material function like multiferroics at room temperature
Source: Emily Ryan, Megan Holtz, Cornell University / USA

Smartphones are now a part of life the world over. To be in a state of constant readiness, however, the battery needs frequent recharging, placing considerable strain on the energy storage medium. According to scientists at the University of Michigan and Cornell University, the use of multiferroic materials will make energy-intensive charging cycles a thing of the past. The scientists have proposed processors for electronic devices that consume 100 times less energy.

A multiferroic material is a substance that is both ferromagnetic and ferroelectric: in a magnetic field it magnetises and in an electric field it changes its polarisation. Until now, substances that exhibit both these effects have only ever been observed at very low temperatures. The researchers in the USA have now succeeded in simulating the permanently magnetic and permanently electrically charged state of a material in a controlled manner, opening up numerous potential applications for electrical devices.

This new material could replace the conventional semiconductors used in current processors, reducing energy consumption to a fraction of today's levels by using pulses of current. The basis of this innovative technology are electroceramics such as barium titanates, which are given various coatings. It is this combination of materials that gives them their multiferroic properties. The researchers are confident that the first small electrical devices such as smartphones and tablet computers based on this new material will soon be available. Such devices will be much more practical for end consumers and also very environmentally friendly.

Projectors in a large-scale test facility generate light radiation with an output of 380 kW
Source: DLR Jülich

SOLAR FUELS

Most experts agree that private transport will in future be powered by electricity generated from renewable energy sources. Larger means of transport such as passenger aircraft, however, require fuels with a higher energy density. For long-haul flights in particular, electric power is not sufficient. A possible remedy could be provided by a kind of artificial sun being developed by scientists at the German Aerospace Center (DLR) in Jülich, with which researchers hope to produce environmentally friendly solar fuels.

Under the name of "Synlight", a test facility with 150 high-performance light units was installed in March 2017, with which aircraft fuel can be extracted from carbon dioxide and water with the aid of a metal catalyst. The lamps, which are normally used in large-scale film projectors, produce light radiation 10,000 times stronger than the solar radiation arriving at the Earth's surface. The large-scale test facility focuses this light in such a way that temperatures of up to 3,500 °C are reached with a maximum power output of 380 kW.

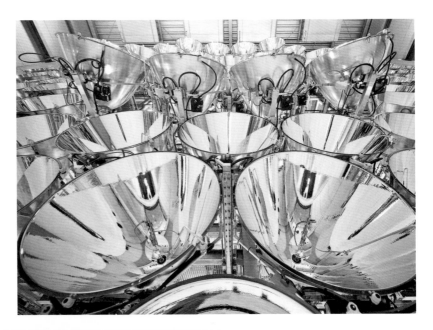

Each lamp has a diameter
of 105 cm
Source: DLR Jülich

In the facility at Jülich, hydrogen, which occurs naturally only as part of a chemical composition, is isolated using a direct chemical process. The xenon short-arc lamps are aligned to focus on one point and form a large artificial sun. By applying this energy, metal is heated up to a temperature of around 800 °C and steam is added causing the metal to oxidise with the oxygen contained in the water vapour. Hydrogen is given off as a result. So far, the process has only been successfully tested in basic research. Work is also underway on the development of a hydrogen-powered aircraft. Dubbed "HY4", it undertook its maiden flight in summer 2016.

ABOUT THE AUTHORS

DR SASCHA PETERS

Dr Sascha Peters is the founder and owner of the futures agency HAUTE INNOVATION based in Berlin. Through his expertise as an innovation consultant, product developer and author, he has become one of the most renowned experts on materials and technology in Europe. Since 1997 Peters has led research projects and product development at the Fraunhofer Institute for Production Technology IPT (Aachen), was deputy director of the Design Zentrum Bremen from 2003 to 2009 and head of the Material Competence Center at Modulor GmbH in Berlin. He gained his doctorate at the University of Duisburg-Essen in 2004 with a thesis on promoting communication between designers and engineers. Peters is the author of numerous specialist publications and lectures widely around the world. Since 2014 he has been a member of the advisory board of the funding initiative "Twenty20 – Partnership for Innovation" on behalf of the German Federal Ministry of Education and Research (BMBF). From 2015 to 2019, Dr Peters was appointed to the jury of the Red Dot Award: Product Design.

DIANA DREWES

Diana Drewes is a cabinet maker by trade and studied product design at Weissensee Academy of Art in Berlin. During her studies she focused on material development utilising natural growth processes and pursued this in her master's degree. In 2017 Drewes joined HAUTE INNOVATION as a materials researcher and materials developer with special expertise in the linking of technology and biology. Diana Drewes has already developed several unique materials that are free of chemicals, consist exclusively of waste materials from the forestry and food industries and are 100% recyclable. In her lectures she presents the latest material innovations based on natural resources and outlines production processes that employ biological processes. She has been a member of the international jury of the 3D Pioneers Challenge since 2016.

INDEX

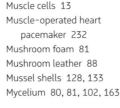

SELECTED PUBLICATIONS
BY THE AUTHORS

03 | 2019
"Mit Kreislaufdenken zu neuen Baumaterialien", Green Critic, md Magazin 3-2019, Verlag Konradin Medien, Stuttgart.

02 | 2019
"Neuen Stoff braucht die Welt", Design Report 1-2019, Rat für Formgebung Medien GmbH, Frankfurt am Main.

09 | 2018
"Additive Fertigung – Der Weg zur individuellen Produktion", Technologieland Hessen, published by: Hessisches Ministerium für Wirtschaft, Energie, Verkehr und Landesentwicklung, Wiesbaden.

08 | 2018
"Stadt als Mine – Wohnmodul im Forschungsgebäude NEST zeigt Wege für die Kreislaufwirtschaft der Zukunft auf", Design Report 4-2018, Rat für Formgebung Medien GmbH, Frankfurt am Main.

06 | 2017
"Fahrt frei für abfallfrei – Materialinnovationen für eine geschlossene Kreislaufwirtschaft", Design Report 3-2017, Rat für Formgebung Medien GmbH, Frankfurt am Main.

04 | 2017
"Textile Exoskelette", Design Report 2-2017, Rat für Formgebung Medien GmbH, Frankfurt am Main.

03 | 2017
"Mit der Natur in die Zukunft. Postindustrielle Produktion mit natürlichen Wachstumsprozessen", context Magazin 1/2017, published by: HeidelbergerCement, Heidelberg.

02 | 2017
"Wiese wird Papier – Gras als alternatives Fasermaterial", Design Report 1-2017, Rat für Formgebung Medien GmbH, Frankfurt am Main.

12 | 2016
"Pilztextil aus Zunderschwamm – Parasiten produzieren Gesundheitsförderliches", Design Report 6-2017, Rat für Formgebung Medien GmbH, Frankfurt am Main.

12 | 2016

"Current Table – Strom von der Scheibe", dds Magazin 12-2016, Verlag Konradin Medien, Stuttgart.

10 | 2016

"Happaratus – Power-Handschuh für den Modellbau", Design Report 5-2016, Rat für Formgebung Medien GmbH, Frankfurt am Main.

8 | 2016

"Fleisch aus der Petrischale – Gezüchtetes In-vitro Fleisch wird kommerzialisiert", Design Report 4-2016, Rat für Formgebung Medien GmbH, Frankfurt am Main.

6 | 2016

"Wasser in Aspik – Biologisch kreislauffähige Alternative zu Plastikflaschen", Design Report 3-2016, Rat für Formgebung Medien GmbH, Frankfurt am Main.

4 | 2016

"ShiftWear Wechselschuhe – Schuhe als Display dank ePaper", Design Report 2-2016, Rat für Formgebung Medien GmbH, Frankfurt am Main.

3 | 2016

"Das Material denkt mit – Smarte Materialien für die Architektur", domus 018 "Die Stadt und der Mensch", ahead media GmbH, Berlin.

2 | 2016

"Moya Power – Flatterndes Minikraftwerk", Design Report 1-2016, Rat für Formgebung Medien GmbH, Frankfurt am Main.

12 | 2015

"Aero Bike – Leichtbau mit Birkenholzlamellen", Design Report 6-2015, Rat für Formgebung Medien GmbH, Frankfurt am Main.

10 | 2015

"Silk Leaf – Eine neue Brise Design", Design Report 5-2015, Rat für Formgebung Medien GmbH, Frankfurt am Main.

9 | 2015

"Die Demokratisierung der Energie – Neuer Markt für Energy Harvesting Produkte und smarte Energiesysteme", Euroscope 3-2015, published by: BASF, Ludwigshafen.

8 | 2015

"Der Traum vom gedruckten Möbel – Potenziale additiver Technologien für die Möbelindustrie", Design Report 4-2015, Rat für Formgebung Medien GmbH, Frankfurt am Main.

6 | 2015

"Wundermaterialien mit auxetischer Struktur", Design Report 3-2015, Rat für Formgebung Medien GmbH, Frankfurt am Main.

4 | 2015

"Additive Fertigung – Der Weg zur individuellen Produktion" (German & English), Nanotech series, published by: Hessisches Ministerium für Wirtschaft, Energie, Verkehr und Landesentwicklung, Wiesbaden.

2 | 2015

"Algen-Biokomposite für Interior- und Möbeldesign", Design Report 1-2015, Rat für Formgebung Medien GmbH, Frankfurt am Main.

10 | 2014

"Organic Waste Design – A New Culture of Designed Waste Porducts" (English & German), chapter in Building from Waste, Birkhäuser Verlag, Basel.

6 | 2014

"Technologie mit Köpfchen – Smart Materials für intelligentes Design", Design Report 3-2014, Verlag Konradin Medien, Stuttgart.

5 | 2014

"Materialien für alle Sinne – Intelligente Werkstoffe für Interior und Design", md Magazin 4-2014, Verlag Konradin Medien, Stuttgart.

2 | 2014

"Holzersatz – Innovative Materialien schonen die Ressourcen", Werkspuren 1-2014, SWV Design und Technik, Schweizerischer Werklehrerinnen- und Werklehrerverein SWV, Zurich.

1 | 2014

Material Revolution II – New Sustainable and Multi-Purpose Materials for Design and Architecture (English & German), Birkhäuser Verlag, Basel.

SELECTED LECTURES
BY THE AUTHORS

21 MAY 2019
"Disruptive Materials", Interzum 2019, Cologne.

26 MARCH 2019
"Zukunftslösungen für intelligente Verpackungen", ISI-Zentrum für Gründung, Business & Innovation, Wirtschaftsförderung im Landkreis Harburg GmbH, Buchholz in der Nordheide.

16 JANUARY 2019
"Design Materials 2019", imm Cologne, Cologne.

14 JANUARY 2019
"3D-Food-Printing und die Nahrungszubereitung der Zukunft", LivingKitchen, Future Foodstyles, Cologne.

29 NOVEMBER 2018
"Werkstofftechnologien für die Zukunft des Bauens", Messe Schulbau, Frankfurt am Main.

16 NOVEMBER 2018
"Graphene-based Innovation", ELMIA Subcontractor, Jönköping/Sweden.

15 NOVEMBER 2018
"3D-Printing of Spare Parts", ELMIA Subcontractor, Jönköping/Sweden.

13 NOVEMBER 2018
"Green Steel: Bamboo, Flax Fiber Composites & Wood Hybrids for the Industry", ELMIA Subcontractor, Jönköping/Sweden.

25 OCTOBER 2018
"Materials Culture – Innovationen einer neuen Werkstoffkultur", Orgatec 2018, Cologne.

12 SEPTEMBER 2018
"Nachhaltige Verpackungsmaterialien von morgen", 1. Kölner Verpackungstag, Cologne.

28 JUNE 2018
"Future Design Materials", HAWK Hildesheim.

26 JUNE 2018

"3D-Drucken im Sanitärbereich: Verfahren, Materialien, Innovationen", GMS Forum 2018, Mainz.

21 JUNE 2018

"Nachhaltige Materialien für eine neue Produktkultur", Institut für Technik, Ressourcenschonung und Energieeffizienz TREE, Hochschule Bonn Rhein-Sieg, Sankt Augustin.

13 JUNE 2018

"Materials Matter – Materialinnovationen für Textil- und Modedesigner", Universität der Künste Berlin.

8 MARCH 2018

"Building Materials from Waste", Ecobuild 2018, WasteZone, ExCel London/UK.

6 MARCH 2018

"4D-Printing und Memory Materials", Eisenwarenmesse 2018, Cologne.

17 FEBRUARY 2018

"3D-Druck im Gesundheitshandwerk", 3D-Druck Anwendertag 2018, Handwerkskammer Berlin.

17 JANUARY 2018

"Materialien für eine dekarbonisierte Produktkultur", imm cologne, Cologne.

16 JANUARY 2018

"Designmaterialien der Zukunft: kreislauffähig, vegan und irgendwie smart", FH Aachen.

15 JANUARY 2018

"Smart Home Materials", imm Cologne, Cologne.

29 NOVEMBER 2017

"Materialien in neuer Dimension – Innovationen für eine dekarbonisierte Gesellschaft", Hochschule Wismar.

28 NOVEMBER 2017

"Smart Materials for Future Construction", TheStadiumBusiness Design & Development Summit 2017, Barcelona/Spain.

27 NOVEMBER 2017

"Multimaterialmix im 3D-Druck", Fachforum "Faszination Kleben", 3M Deutschland, Neuss.

23 NOVEMBER 2017

"Plastics in Progress – Neue Materialien für die Kunststoffindustrie", INNONET Innovationstag 2017, Horb am Neckar.

17 NOVEMBER 2017

"Sustainable Materials für Eco Design", ELMIA Subcontractor, Jönköping/Sweden.

15 NOVEMBER 2017

"4D-Printing und die Potentiale für die Automobilindustrie und die Luftfahrt", ELMIA Subcontractor, Jönköping/Sweden.

2 NOVEMBER 2017

"4D-Printing: Anwendungspotenziale für die Zukunft der Mobilität", Event: Additive Fertigung für die Mobilität, Tatcraft, Frankfurt am Main.

26 OCTOBER 2017

"Building from Waste – Bauwerkstoffe aus Abfallmaterialien", KIT Karlsruher Institut für Technologie – Fachgebiet Nachhaltiges Bauen, Karlsruhe.

19 OCTOBER 2017

"Smart Stones", Marble Show, Antalya Expo Center, Antalya/Turkey.

17 OCTOBER 2017

"Bautechnologien und Materialinnovationen für die smarte Serie", 17. Fassadentag, FORUM Haus der Architekten, Stuttgart.

12 OCTOBER 2017

"Future Fibers for a Circular Economy", 2nd Circular Economy Conference, Aarhus University, Campus Herning/Denmark.

29 SEPTEMBER 2017

"Future of Metal Printing", XERION Innovation Day 2017, Berlin.

20 JUNE 2017

"Potenziale des 4D-Printings", 3D Printing Conference, FabCon 3.D, Messe Erfurt.

18 MAY 2017

"Infungitum – Endlos Reproduktion", Circular Thinking-Conference, Interzum, Cologne.

15 MAY 2017

"Werkstoffe der Zukunft", 6. Innovationsworkshop Holzwerkstoffe, Interzum, Cologne.

6 APRIL 2017

"Materialtrends für die Automobilindustrie 2017", Donne e Mobile, Internationales Netzwerkevent der Fahrzeugdesignerinnen, Milan/Italy.

4 APRIL 2017
"Materialinnovationen wandeln die Gesellschaft", Swiss eLearning Conference 2017, Messe Zurich/Switzerland.

28 MARCH 2017
"Generatives Design: Potenziale des 3D-Drucks und der additiven Fertigung für Designer", Deutsches Fachkolloquium Textil, RWTH Aachen.

14 MARCH 2017
"3D-Druck fürs Bad", ISH, Messe Frankfurt, Frankfurt am Main.

6 FEBRUARY 2017
"Material Innovation for Responsible Growth", 12th HSBC Conference, Frankfurt am Main.

18 JANUARY 2017
"Material Trends 2017", imm Cologne, Cologne.

24 NOVEMBER 2016
"Materialinnovationen für Zukunftstechnologien", HSBC Investorenfrühstück, Amsterdam/Netherlands.

11 NOVEMBER 2016
"Smart Materials für effiziente Lösungen in Konstruktion und Design", ELMIA Subcontractor, Jönköping/Sweden.

10 NOVEMBER 2016
"Materialinnovationen für die additive Produktion und den 3D-Druck", ELMIA Subcontractor, Jönköping/Sweden.

25 OCTOBER 2016
"Smart Office Materials", Orgatec Speakers' Corner, Cologne.

22 JUNE 2016
"Kunststoffinnovationen mit alternativen Rohstoffquellen", Pro-K Tagung, dbb forum Berlin.

15 JUNE 2016
"Additive Produktion für die Möbelindustrie – Potenziale für Designer und Unternehmen", FabCon 3.D Conference, Messe Erfurt.

5 MAY 2016
"Smart Materials for Smart Design", 5th Int. Interior Architecture Symposium, Mimar Sinan University, Istanbul/Turkey.

31 MARCH 2016

"AUDI Designtalk: Von der Vision zur Serie", AUDI City Berlin.

10 MARCH 2016

"The Next Big Thing – Additive Manufacturing and 3D Printing for the Design and Furniture Industry", Interior Designer Day, Singapore Design Week, Singapore.

14 JANUARY 2016

"Kunststoffinnovationen für eine dekarbonisierte Gesellschaft", Pro-K Innovationspreis, Frankfurt am Main.

20 NOVEMBER 2015

"Smarte Energiesysteme der Zukunft", Designathon "Energy2Go", Creator Space Tour 2015, BASF Ludwigshafen.

19 NOVEMBER 2015

"Materialinnovationen für generatives Design", formnext design dialog, Messe Frankfurt.

18 NOVEMBER 2015

"Biobasierte und nachhaltige Materiallösungen für smartes Design", Conference "Smart Materials for Future Design", Red Dot Design Museum, Zeche Zollverein, Essen.

13 NOVEMBER 2015

"Smart Energy Materials – Energy Harvesting für eine regenerative Energieversorgung", ELMIA Subcontractor, Jönköping/Sweden.

10 NOVEMBER 2015

"Biobasierte Materialien und Leichtbau-Lösungen für die industrielle Zulieferindustrie", ELMIA Subcontractor, Jönköping/Sweden.

17 SEPTEMBER 2015

"Materials Revolution – Neue Werkstoffe für zukünftiges Bauen", Erbe Medizintechnik, Tübingen.

3 JULY 2015

"Designing Materials – Technologie-Innovationen durch Kreative", designxport, Hamburg.

29 JUNE 2015

"Future Thinking Materials", School of Form, Poznań/Poland.

15 MAY 2015

"Textile Innovationen – Nachhaltige und smarte Materialtechnologien für die Textilindustrie", Veredlertag 2015, Friedrichshafen.

8 MAY 2015
"Weben, Drucken, Züchten: Textilinnovationen für das nächste Jahrzehnt", Polster &
Bedding Workshop, Interzum, Cologne.

25 APRIL 2015
"Smart Materials und intelligente Oberflächen", Fraunhofer Smart Materials Day,
Dresden.

23 APRIL 2015
"Innovationen und Impulse für eine nachhaltige Stadtentwicklung", KANN Dialog
2015, Cologne.

7 APRIL 2015
"Zukunftslabor für nachhaltige Produktentwicklung", Haus der Industrie, Vienna/
Austria.

24 FEBRUARY 2015
"Neue Werkstofflösungen und Materialinnovationen für das Zeitalter der Bioökono-
mie", Audi-Innovationsnetzwerk der Produktion, Ingolstadt.

5 FEBRUARY 2015
"Materielle Revolution – Nachhaltige und smarte Werkstoffe für Architektur und
Design", Architekturforum Zurich/Switzerland.

10 DECEMBER 2014
"Materials Revolution – Innovative materials and their implementation as a progres-
sing tool in the architectural work", The international Convention for Innovation in
Design and Architecture, Tel Aviv/Israel.

27 NOVEMBER 2014
"Generative Produktion im 21. Jahrhundert", EuroMold, Frankfurt am Main.

20 NOVEMBER 2014
"Innovationen für die gedruckte Gesellschaft – Vom Beginn einer neuen Produktions-
kultur", IHK Industrieausschuss, Laser Zentrum Nord, Hamburg.

19 NOVEMBER 2014
"Neue Materialien für die additive Fertigung", Anwenderforum "Rapid Product
Development", Fraunhofer IPA, Stuttgart.

13 NOVEMBER 2014
"Smart Engineering Materials – Smart Solutions for Advanced Products", ELMIA Subcontractor, Jönköping/Sweden.

11 NOVEMBER 2014
"Materials Revolution – Sustainable and lightweight materials for engineering and design", ELMIA Subcontractor, Jönköping/Sweden.

25 OCTOBER 2014
"Biologisches Design für Möbelbau und Interior", Orgatec Speakers' Corner, Cologne.

30 SEPTEMBER 2014
"Die generative Revolution – Innovationen für die gedruckte Gesellschaft", ISI-Zentrum für Gründung, Business & Innovation, Buchholz in der Nordheide.

19 JULY 2014
"Nachhaltigkeit als Trend in der Textilproduktion", Mercedes-Benz Fashion Studio, Bikini Berlin.

26 JUNE 2014
"Smart and Sustainable Materials for Automotive Interiors", Automotive Interiors Expo 2014, Messe Stuttgart.

23 MAY 2014
"Smart Textiles Revolution: Nachhaltige und intelligente Materialien für innovatives Textil- und Modedesign", 5. Symposium "GREEN CYCLES – Corporate Social Responsibility im Textilen Kreislauf", HAW Hamburg.

19 MAY 2014
"Smart Office Materials", INDEX design talks, INDEX International Design Exhibition, Dubai World Trade Center, United Arab Emirates.

16 MAY 2014
"Textile Revolution – Nachhaltige Materialien für die Faser- und Bekleidungsindustrie", MG OPEN SPACES – Nachhaltigkeit in der Textil- und Bekleidungsindustrie, Hochschule Niederrhein, Krefeld.

29 APRIL 2014
"Bio-basierte Materialien für eine nachhaltige Industrie des 21. Jahrhunderts", STERN-Forum "Innovation and Biomaterials", Haus der Wirtschaft, Stuttgart.

14 APRIL 2014
"Ungewöhnliche Materialien für nachhaltiges Produktdesign", Kulturstiftung des Bundes, Halle an der Saale.

4 APRIL 2014
"Smart Office Materials – Werkstoffinnovationen für die Büromöbelindustrie", Spanischer Hof, Gröditz.

16 JANUARY 2014

"Gutes Morgen – Materialien für eine nachhaltige Zukunft", Salon D, Passagen-Programm der imm Cologne, Cologne.

10 JANUARY 2014

"Materials World – Innovationen für die Produktkultur des 21. Jahrhunderts", Staged Conference, room & style Messe Dresden.

ACKNOWLEDGEMENTS

We would like to thank all the developers and innovators, scientists and producers, architects and designers who have supported and inspired us with their in-depth knowledge and numerous references to previously unpublished works on new materials. Without their contribution, we would not have been able to present such an extensive range of different material developments.

We are likewise indebted to Birkhäuser Verlag, who once again have given us the opportunity to publish a new book on current advances in material development for a wider audience. Special thanks go to Henriette Mueller-Stahl and her team for their competent support in bringing this book to fruition.

Diana Drewes and Sascha Peters